Biscuiteers Book of Iced Cookies

Harriet Hastings co-founded Biscuiteers with
Stevie Congdon and is also a co-director of
leading London catering company Lettice.
She is the mother of four young Biscuiteers.

Sarah Moore is a Creative Director, connoisseur
of delicious cookies, self-confessed vintage
addict, and mother of three fine young Biscuiteers.

D1401573

Biscuiteers Book of Iced Cookies

Harriet Hastings & Sarah Moore

Photography by Katie Hammond

Kyle Books

This book is very largely thanks to the flair and talent of some very important people:

Victoria Sawdon, book designer, artistic director, and talented illustrator who designs and illustrates all Biscuiteers tins.

Sarah Moore, co-author, cookie designer, and creative consultant.

Marion Piffaut, our production manager who supervised production of the cookies and generally makes everything happen.

Rina Wanti, Ceridwen Olofson, and Belinda Chen, who iced the cookies for the book.

Katie Hammond, our talented photographer.

Perry Haydn Taylor, Bill Barlow, and everyone at Big Fish, our design agency and partners, for all their energy, creativity, and brilliance, and for letting us use their studio a lot.

Stevie Congdon, head of all Biscuiteers production, husband, partner, and the fourth Biscuiteer.

Kyle Cathie, Judith Hannam, and Vicky Orchard at Kyle Cathie for helping us produce a book we are all really proud of.

And finally to all the other Biscuiteers—our icers, bakers, office staff, and, most importantly, customers, who have helped to make it all happen.

Kyle Books
www.kylebooks.com
Distributed by National Book Network
4501 Forbes Blvd. Suite 200
Lanham, MD 20706
(800) 462-6420

First published in Great Britain by Kyle Books

ISBN 978-1-906868-37-6

Library of Congress Control Number: 2011926472

Text © Biscuiteer Baking Company Ltd 2010. www.biscuiteers.com
Design © Kyle Cathie Limited 2010
Photographs © Katie Hammond 2010 except page 8 © Edward Hill
and page 47 © Peter Cassidy

All rights reserved. No reproduction, copy or transmission of this publication may be made without written permission. No paragraph of this publication may be reproduced, copied or transmitted save with written permission or in accordance with the provisions of the Copyright Act 1956 (as amended). Any person who does any unauthorised act in relation to this publication may be liable to criminal prosecution and civil claims for damages.

Editor: Vicky Orchard
Design: Victoria Sawdon at Big Fish
Photography: Katie Hammond
Styling: Liz Belton
Food styling: Sarah Moore
Cookie Production: Marion Piffaut
Copy editor: Clare Hubbard
Production: Gemma John

Color reproduction by Scanhouse in Malaysia
Printed in China by C&C Offset Printing Co., Ltd.

Contents

Introduction

We came up with the idea for Biscuiteers on a weekend in New York. We were sure that there were lots of people who are as passionate about cookies as we are and that there was a real opportunity to set up a cookie gift business online that was completely different from anything else in the market—cookies that would look as beautiful as they tasted. In fact, cookies that people would want to talk about. It was on that trip that we were inspired by some of the cookies we found and realized that we hadn't seen anything like them at home.

We started planning Biscuiteers properly in spring of 2007, testing our cookie recipes in Stevie's catering kitchens. We baked batch after batch to develop our own core flavors—chocolate, vanilla, and allspice. From the start we were committed to using the very best natural ingredients to get the flavor we wanted. We then started planning our launch collections, working on our designs, and deciding on the big occasions. We wanted the cookies to be beautiful and witty since, from the start, we saw them as an adult gift. We called them "collections" because we knew we wanted to launch them seasonally like fashion collections and to keep refreshing and developing the range to ensure our customers kept coming back. It was important that we found our own style—distinctive designs that would make our cookies instantly recognizable. We created our original cookies on paper first and then by icing them onto parchment paper.

There were lots of teething problems! It took us a while to work out how to dry the icing to the right degree to ensure that the cookies didn't become soggy. It took us a bit longer to work out how to secure the cookies in the tins to make sure they didn't arrive broken or chipped.

Biscuiteers launched online in September 2007 with our mission statement, "why send flowers when you can send cookies instead?" The media seemed to get it immediately and were very taken with our launch fashion collections, which remain some of our bestselling lines. Suddenly we had orders, lots of them. It became apparent that we couldn't continue to camp in Stevie's catering kitchens and office. We moved into our first bakery in November 2007.

There was lots of interest in Biscuiteers, and we started selling in the department store Selfridges in January 2008—not just our tin collections but our cookie cards. We very much wanted to have a simple single cookie product on the website and came up with the idea of a cookie greeting card—more than a card but less than a tin. These have really taken off in London and we now sell in Harrods, Fortnum & Mason, Liberty, Fenwick, and John Lewis. We also send lots of cookies overseas. You will find them in Galeries Lafayettes, Colette and La Grande Épicerie in France and as far afield as Dubai and Greece.

One of the real joys of iced cookies is their incredible flexibility. Our experienced designers do some wonderful work copying logos and fashion designs and all sorts of products. We have had some exciting commissions, including a collaboration with Anya Hindmarch to create a tin of her handbags and a circus tin exclusively for the Conran shop. We designed a limited-edition tin to celebrate Selfridges' 100th birthday and custom cookies for the launch of Harvey Nichols' 4th floor. The cookies are used for press launches, iced place names and cookie card invitations, or party bags. We have created custom designs for outstanding brands such as Mulberry, Boden, Swatch, and Fit Flop, among many others.

We also do a lot of custom work for private parties, weddings, christenings, baby showers, and birthday parties, and we have shared lots of our favorite designs with you in this book. There is nothing more rewarding than creating a tin for a friend's birthday with all their special things.

The business has grown but we still make and ice our biscuits in exactly the same way. They are all handmade, and part of the excitement has been building a business based on old-fashioned, non-industrialized techniques. Many of our icers are artists and enjoy creating new designs and perfecting existing ones as much as we do. Each cookie is lovingly made from start to finish, and each one is totally individual.

In this book, we have shared some of our icing secrets with you. Everyone can create their own cookies at home, many of which are really very simple, and they do make wonderful gifts for children and adults. Icing is fun for everybody, and you can really let your artistic streak run wild—there is no limit to the possibilities or the designs. We have given detailed guides to some of our most popular collections to show you how to create the same effects in easy-to-follow, step-by-step guides. We have also included a chapter on packaging and mailing to help you share your creations with family and friends. We hope that, after reading this, you will want to become a Biscuiteer, too!

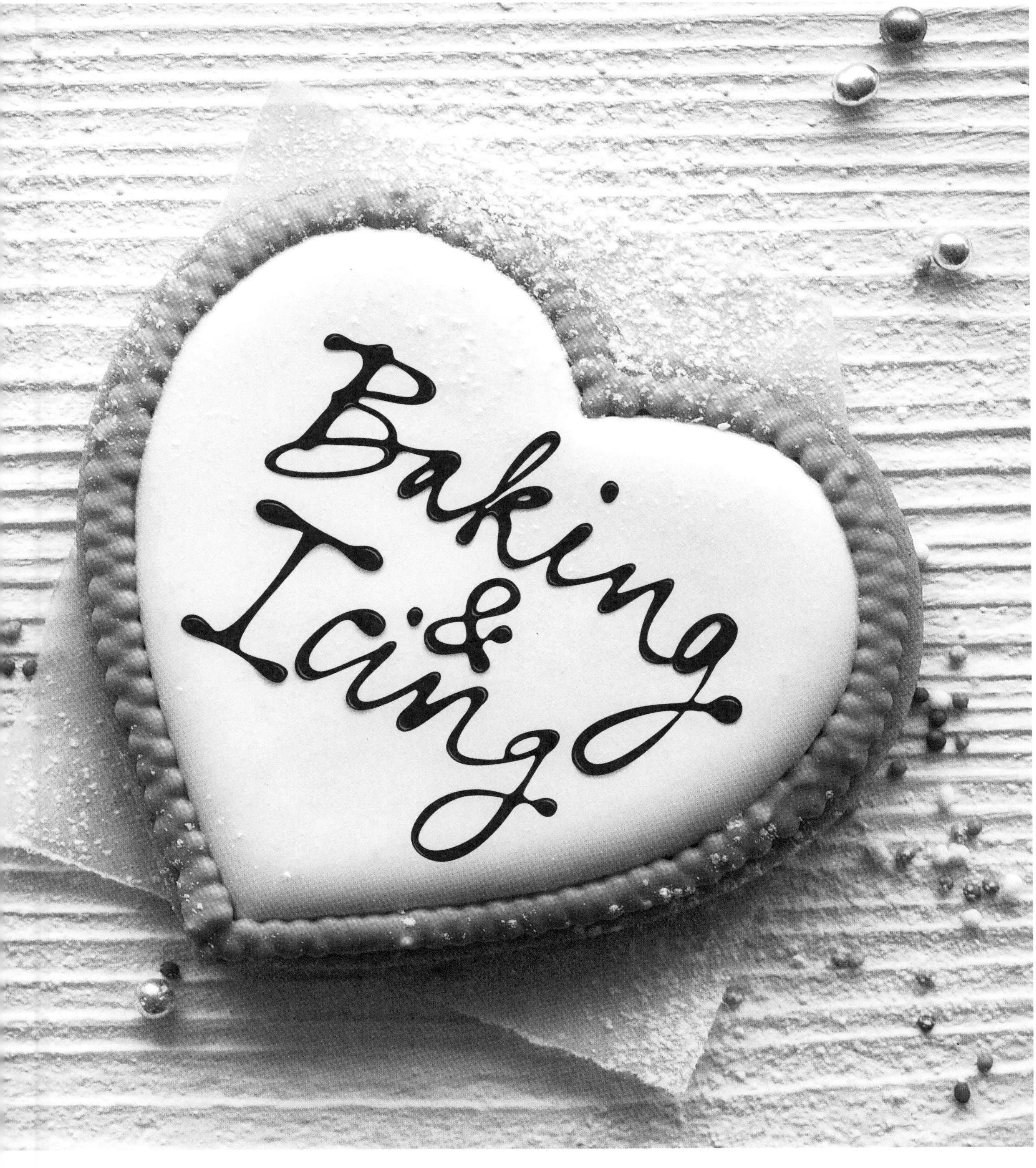
Baking
&
Icing

The Golden Rules of Cookie Making

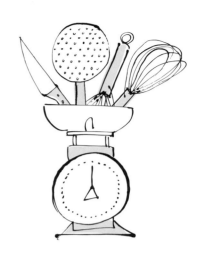

At Biscuiteers' baking HQ, we are very lucky to have a beautiful big kitchen, with lots of shiny steel tables, fridges, handy racks that roll on little wheels, and marvelous mixers that make cookie making a real pleasure. We handmake lovely batches of all the cookie dough and icing that we use, and we get to have great fun baking and icing every day. But when we come to do it at home, we have to remember that there are some things that help to make the process go a little more smoothly.

Make a plan: it can take quite a long time to make your cookie dough: roll it, chill it, cut it, bake it, cool it, mix icings, pipe and fill, and add sprinkles or decorations; so make a plan, particularly if children are involved. Perhaps make and bake cookies one day, and make icings and pipe another day. All baked cookies made from our basic cookie recipes (see pages 32–39) can be kept in airtight containers for at least a week, and the icing can be made in advance, although it is easiest to use on the day that it is made.

Clear away: before you start to bake it is really helpful to clear and clean a work surface area large enough for you to roll out the cookie dough on.

Cover up: a big apron and rolled-up or short sleeves help to prevent you from getting icing on your clothes. We use a mixture of natural powder colors derived from, among other things, beets and carrots, and gel colors that are widely available. At the end of every day, there is always a rainbow of colors on our aprons. But be careful because the colors can stain clothes and fabric, and sometimes even people's mouths!

Little ones: make sure that any little helpers are kept well away from any mixers, machines, and hot ovens or are carefully supervised if they want to be involved in the fun.

Chill out: make some room in the fridge because cookie dough needs to relax somewhere cool before it is baked. Make enough room for a baking sheet and then stack the sheets one on top of the other if you are making lots of cookies.

Preparation: have a good look at the ingredients and any special equipment that you need to make your chosen cookies, and gather it all together before you begin. Keep things simple to start with if you are new to icing and decorating.

Quality matters: use good-quality ingredients; their use makes a difference to the flavor of the cookie.

Practice: you can practice icing onto sheets of wax paper before you commit to decorating your precious handmade cookies. Or perhaps buy a package of cookies and practice on these until you are more confident; pick ones that are as smooth and level on the top as possible.

Weights and measures: read the recipes and icing guidelines all the way through before you begin. Follow the instructions carefully and make sure that you have good measuring cups and spoons or accurate scales on which to weigh all your ingredients. Remember: when coloring icing you can always add more color, but you can't take it away.

At Biscuiteers we mainly ice our cookies with royal icing. Traditionally it is made from beating egg whites and confectioner's sugar together for a long time until a thick, smooth, white paste is formed.

Egg whites: lots of recipes use fresh egg whites but we always use a dried egg-white substitute for our cookies. It is available in most supermarkets and is easier and safer to use than fresh egg whites as it removes the risk of salmonella that can be found in fresh eggs. You can also buy royal icing mix: a prepared combination of confectioners' sugar and dried egg whites that simply needs the right amount of water added to it. Finally, you can also make up the icing using pasteurized liquid egg white. (See Suppliers on page 157 for full details of where these products are available.) Icing made from any of these ingredients tastes pretty much the same, so choose the one that you find easiest or most convenient to prepare.

We use two basic types of royal icing: a thick, smooth paste for piping details and edging, and a runnier glossy mixture for flooding larger areas.

Piping icing: this needs to be smooth and thick, a bit like the texture of toothpaste. It has to be just soft enough to squeeze out of the piping bag, but also thick enough to hold its shape perfectly.

This icing is used for piping borders, which form little "walls" around the areas of the cookie that you want to fill with the flooding icing, and for adding fine detail and decoration.

Flooding icing: just about pourable, thicker than heavy cream, this glossy icing is squeezed onto cookies to flood areas where a shiny, smooth effect is required. It is well worth investing in a few little squeezy bottles to dispense this icing from. With their screw-on nozzles, they are perfect for directing the flow of flooding icing to exactly where it should be.

Remember that making icing is not an exact science. Even though we have a tried-and-tested method of making our icing, we often end up adding a little more water or confectioners' sugar to get the icing to exactly the right consistency.

Equipment: all icing needs to be made with spotlessly clean and dry equipment, because even tiny amounts of grease can affect how the egg whites whip up and how thick the icing becomes. You can make royal icing by hand but it is much easier if you have an electric beater or food processor. If you are making it by hand, combine your chosen ingredients in a mixing bowl and beat for about 10 minutes until you have a lovely bright-white smooth paste.

Additions: adding color and flavor to the icing affects the consistency, so start with the thickest icing that you need and always add water, color, and flavorings a little at a time.

For best results: you really need to use icing on the day that it is made. Keep it in an airtight container or cover it in the bowl in which it was made as soon as you have transformed it into the type, color, and flavor required. It can be stored in the fridge in piping bags or squeezy bottles for up to three days, but both types of icing separate a little and become less easy to handle on standing for a long time.

Drying cookies: when you have iced the details, added the baubles, and sprinkled on the glitter, you might find that the moisture in the icing has affected the crunchiness of the cookie. At Biscuiteers we return all of our cookies to the oven at a very low temperature for about 30 minutes to make sure that they are all totally dry. So put them back into a warm oven on baking sheets to dry off. Smaller cookies, or ones with just a little iced line detail, won't take very long at all.

Finally: even at Biscuiteers, where we ice and bake all day every day, we still manage to make quite a few cookies that don't turn out just the way they should. Always aim to make a few more than you need and enjoy the odd imperfect cookie along the way.

Dough Making

At Biscuiteers we have tried and tested all sorts of recipes in the pursuit of a delicious, easy-to-make, and easy-to-use cookie dough. In this section are our favorite recipes, made from natural ingredients and using real flavors.

In each of the collections we recommend the dough that goes well with the cookies being made, but these are only suggestions, and if you love only the Super Chocolatey variety (see page 34) or you have your own recipe, that's fine, too. Whichever one you choose, bear in mind that you need a dough that rolls out easily, cooks evenly, and is suitable for cutting. Big chunks of chocolate, whole cranberries, or hazelnuts taste delicious but make it difficult to cut and ice evenly.

helpful hints for dough making

* Read through the whole recipe before you start.

* Check that your scales are accurate from time to time (test them with a can of baked beans or something similar that has a given weight).

* Measure all your ingredients carefully before you begin.

* Take the butter out of the fridge 15–30 minutes (depending on the temperature of your kitchen) before you begin as it will be easier to use.

* When making your dough, try not to handle it any more than you need to as this makes it tough.

* You can make the dough by hand in a big mixing bowl or use a food processor with the paddle (sometimes called the K-beater) attachment, not the whisk. Remember to start the process on the lowest setting so that the kitchen is not filled with clouds of flour.

* Clear a nice big space on the worktop before rolling and have ready at least two baking sheets covered with a sheet of parchment paper for each batch of cookies to chill and cook on.

Dough Rolling & Keeping

Your dough will be most easy to roll directly after you have made it, as it is naturally softer and more pliable at this point. (If you want to make the dough ahead of time, roll it into two flat disks, cover with plastic wrap, and refrigerate. Bring to room temperature when you need to use it.) Adding flour to help roll out the dough makes it tougher. The trick is to roll it between two sheets of parchment paper. This means you don't have to use any extra flour at all, so this is a technique worth perfecting.

* Divide the dough in two and shape into two flat disks.

* Place the dough on a sheet of baking parchment.

* To make your dough as even as possible you can use rolling guides; you can buy these from specialist shops. Or improvise by using a couple of wooden spoons.

* Begin by gently squashing the dough down with the rolling pin or your hands, cover with a second sheet of parchment, and and then use the rolling pin to roll properly.

* The top sheet of paper may crinkle from time to time. Just peel it off and smooth it down gently and start rolling again.

* Gently roll the dough until it is a quarter-inch thick all over.

* Transfer the whole sheet of rolled dough still sandwiched between its sheets of parchment to a baking sheet and place in the fridge to chill for at least 20–30 minutes before cutting.

* Repeat the process with the rest of the dough.

cutting, cooking, cooling, & keeping

So much time and effort goes into making these cookies that it is important to look after them carefully at every stage of their production. Keep a close eye on the first couple of batches you cook until you get used to your oven and the recipes.

* Assemble your collection of cutters or templates and start to cut. To use the dough efficiently, cut the cookies out as close together as possible. Lift each cookie onto the parchment-covered baking sheet and make sure they are not too close together as the dough will spread a little on baking. Any trimmings can be rerolled a couple of times.

* Preheat the oven to 350°F before you begin making your cookies.

* Evenly space the baking sheets in the oven and cook for 14–18 minutes, depending on your oven.

* When the cookies are evenly cooked and just beginning to turn a golden color (you can't see this on the Super Chocolatey ones [see page 34] but they begin to darken slightly), remove the baking sheets from the oven, and transfer the whole sheet of parchment to a cooling rack or lift each cookie off with a spatula. Do this carefully as the cookies will be quite fragile and hot!

* Cool totally before storing or they will lose their crunch, and don't ice the cookies while they are still warm as the icing will melt.

* Store the cooked, cooled cookies between layers of parchment in an airtight tin or plastic container. They will keep like this for up to a week, if you can resist them.

Basic Royal Icing

ingredients:

powdered egg-white recipe

¾ cup water

2lbs, 3oz / 8 cups confectioners' sugar

1oz egg-white powder

all-in-one recipe

⅔ cup cold water

2lb royal icing mix

egg-white recipe

4 egg whites (see package for details of measuring out your egg whites)

2lbs, 3oz / 8 cups confectioners' sugar

We use royal icing to ice all of our cookies. Before you begin, assemble all of the ingredients and colors together that you need. Remember to use spotlessly clean equipment and familiarize yourself with the Golden Rules.

* All of the recipes are prepared in the same way. Combine all the ingredients in a mixing bowl, starting with the liquids first.

* Add the dry ingredients and whisk or beat for about 5 minutes if using an electric beater or whisk, or for longer if using a wooden spoon. Whisk slowly to start with to avoid clouds of confectioners' sugar covering you and your kitchen.

* Continue whisking until the ingredients form a thick, smooth paste that is bright white in color and has the consistency of toothpaste.

* If you are not using immediately, cover the surface of the icing with plastic wrap to stop it from drying out and refrigerate.

practice makes perfect icing

It can take a while to get used to icing. When we first started, sometimes we would be concentrating so hard on what was coming out of the pointed end of the piping bag, we failed to notice it was all spilling out of the top! And to this day, for every batch of cookies we make, there are always a few that don't make the grade. We have noticed, however, that the cookies that are misshapen or the ones with the wiggly lines or colorful splotches taste just as good as the perfect ones…

As it takes a lot of time and effort and ingredients to make cookies, we often introduce our Biscuiteers to icing by placing outlines of the cookie under sheets of parchment. Like a "tracing paper" for cooks, parchment can be laid over any design to help you get a feel for icing, and you can get a good idea of the pattern and the shape that you want to make on your finished cookies. Have a look at the iced decorations on page 31 to see what else you can do with parchment.

With most of our designs, you need to use a combination of line and flooding icing to create the patterns. The line icing is used to make a little "wall" around the section of cookie that you want to fill with the flooding icing, and to add details and decorations to the surface of the cookie.

When you have filled the icing bags with your chosen colors, you are ready to begin.

Preparing and Coloring Icing

Once you have made your basic royal icing, you are now ready to make up your icing palette. This means that you need to prepare the flooding icing and the colors that you're going to need for your chosen cookies. Check the key on the collection that you are icing, or make up your own color palette.

At Biscuiteers we use some fantastic powdered colors that are derived from plants. They come in all sorts of colors and are made from carrots and beets, spinach and red cabbage, but for home baking, other options are easier to find.

The traditional bottles of food coloring in most supermarkets are suitable for basic coloring, but for a more interesting palette the food-color gels are really useful and are pretty much essential if you want strong colors, particularly red and black.

Most cookshops stock a range, and you can start with a few basic colors and add other colors as you need them.

Most of the cookies we make use the two types of icing mentioned in the Golden Rules—line and flooding icing (see opposite). For each collection you will usually need about a third of your royal icing mixture to make the line colors and the remaining two-thirds for flooding icing. There are a few exceptions so check the individual collections before you begin. It is worth saving a little plain icing of each texture just in case you need any extra colors or need to make up some more of a particular color.

Line Icing

* Check to see how many colors of line icing you need and then divide up the icing. Spoon required amounts into clean little bowls (or you can use pots, teacups, mugs, etc.).

* If you are using gel colors, use the tip of a toothpick to add a tiny amount of the gel to the icing. Stir the gel into the icing until it is totally mixed in and you see the resulting color.

* Slowly add more gel, stirring well between additions, until the color has reached the shade that you need. It is worth taking the coloring process slowly as a little gel color goes a very long way!

* Cover the surface of the icing with plastic wrap, and chill each bowl as you make it until you have all the colors that you need for the collection.

Bottled liquid food coloring is a lot less intense than the gels, but you still need to add it gradually a drop at a time. You cannot achieve intense shades with liquid colors, but they work fine for pastel shades. You may need to beat in a little extra confectioners' sugar if the liquid color begins to thin down your line icing.

You can also try adding your own natural flavors and colors. Whatever you choose, remember that the icing needs to be super smooth, and adding any fresh ingredients may affect its setting and keeping qualities. Try coffee; cocoa powder; raspberry, cherry, or blackberry purée; lemon or orange zest.

Flooding Icing

The rest of the mixture is used to make flooding icing.

* Place it in a large bowl, gradually add enough water, a few drops at a time, stirring constantly, until you have a smooth, just pourable mixture that has roughly the same consistency as heavy cream.

* Repeat the coloring process with the flooding icing. Look at your designs and count up the number of shades of flooding icing needed. Divide up the mixture, leaving a little spare white icing just in case you need to make any extra later.

* When you have finished, cover the surface of each icing with plastic wrap as soon as you have mixed it so that the icing does not start to go hard at the edges, and chill until ready to use.

These are most of the colors that we use and that appear in the collections
top row: grape, eucalyptus, baby blue, Aegean blue, leaf green, sage green, donkey brown
second row: violet, parma violet, gray, deep-sea blue, forest green, pea green, lime green

third row: ivory, hydrangea, strawberry mousse, gentian blue, fuchsia, rose, primrose, black
bottom row: white, baby pink, raspberry, red, orange, mustard yellow, bright yellow

Piping Bags & Squeezy Bottles

You are now ready to put your line icing into piping bags, and there are several different types that you can use.

Reusable fabric varieties, also called pastry bags: available from cookshops, these are used with piping nozzles and fittings. You can use them for icing, but be warned: they may take on the color of the icing you are using; small ones are fine as you normally don't need more than a couple of spoonfuls of each icing.

Paper cones: these are the standard option for most experienced cake decorators. Made by folding a triangle of parchment paper into a perfect cone shape, they can be created at home, and you can use them with or without a nozzle.

Make your own: you can make a simple cone from wax paper. Secure the end with a little clear tape or fold over the top as in the picture below.

Disposable plastic icing bags: at Biscuiteers we use these all the time. You can store your icing in them in the fridge, work with them without having to use piping nozzles, and you can instantly see what color icing is inside.

Nozzles: these are the plastic or metal cones that you put in the end of a piping bag to alter the pattern or type of flow of the icing you are using. They are essential if you are using the reusable fabric variety of piping bag. Normally you push a larger plastic cone inside the bag and then attach your piping nozzle to this from the outside.

For the paper and plastic icing bags, you can just snip a tiny triangle off the tip of the bag to create a minuscule hole in the end and make perfect lines without a nozzle. Alternatively, you can snip a half inch or so off the end and use with a nozzle. This is useful if you want to make different types of pattern with the icing, such as ribbons, leaves, or star shapes.

Filling an icing bag:

* Choose the type of bag that you want to use and pop in a nozzle (if using).

* Stand the bag upright in a suitable container (jar, mug, etc.).

* Carefully spoon the icing into the bag. Use a flexible spatula to scoop up all the icing from the bowl. Don't overfill—you can always refill later.

* When the bag is two-thirds full, pick it up and squeeze the icing down to the bottom of the bag and twist or clip the top shut. (We use those little plastic clips that you can use to keep cereal packs closed, but you can also use rubber bands. Paper cones can be folded shut, too).

* If you have not used a nozzle, you are now ready to snip the end off the piping bag and begin to ice. Start by cutting the smallest tip off straight across the bag. If you cut at an angle, you will create oval lines of icing rather than round. So make sure it is straight!

Squeezy bottles: these are readily available to buy online or in cake-decorating shops. If you can, buy several of these since using just one will be incredibly time-consuming and inconvenient. They come in many different sizes; several small ones are ideal as you are sometimes dealing with quite small quantities of icing. The standard ones come with their own simple nozzle attached. The advantages of these bottles is that they stand upright and the icing does not pour out, you can store the icing in the fridge and it doesn't dry out, and they are really helpful in directing just the right amount of icing to just the right place.

* Fill the bottle carefully using a spatula to guide the flow through the wide neck.

* Attach a nozzle to the bottle if it has one, or simply snip off the flexible plastic nozzle to alter the flow of the icing from the bottle.

Icing a line: hold the bag in two hands and gently squeeze the icing down toward the tip of the bag with your top hand and direct its flow with the other hand. * With the tip of the bag just above the surface of the cookie, but not touching, squeeze evenly and slowly until you create a little trail. Stop squeezing for a second and the trail will stop.

Outlines: if you are making an outline to fill with flooding icing, you need to make sure that you connect your trail to form an unbroken wall around the shape you need. If there are any gaps, the flooding icing will flow through. When you first start, or if you are icing with children, either choose a larger plain nozzle (No. 3) or cut a larger hole in the end of the bag so that you ice a thicker wall. Let the "walls" dry for about 5 minutes before filling with flooding icing.

Flooding: at Biscuiteers we squeeze our flooding icing in place using little clear plastic squeezy bottles (see page 27). For very fine details where only a tiny area needs to be flooded, it is easier to use a little piping bag. Fill them in just the same way as with line icing (see page 23), but be careful as the icing will pour out of both ends if left unsecured! * For simple designs, or when you are starting out, you can just spoon the icing onto the cookies and spread it out using a toothpick or little skewer. * Remember to return your cookies to the oven when they are finished—see note on page 15 about drying cookies.

Flood on flood: this is a delightfully simple and very effective way of decorating. You can make polka dots, stripes, flowers, or any design that requires a smooth and glossy pattern. Fill an outline until only just full with flooding icing and immediately ice your patterns onto the surface using more flooding icing. If you initially overfill the cookie, when you add the detail sometimes the icing breaks over the little walls you have made like a burst dam and you end up having to eat the cookie immediately! Ice the cookies one at a time so that the background is wet and the details can "melt" into the surface.

Line on flood: this is perfect for adding detail to your cookies. Wait until the flooding icing is completely dry and then pipe on the details with line icing.

Glitter and sparkling sugar: there are some styles of cookie that look just great with a little extra sparkle. There are all sorts of edible glitters on the market to help you add that special twinkle. As a general rule, less is more! Remember that the glitter and sugar will stick to any icing that is still wet. So either allow the cookie to dry completely and then pipe on a line where you want the glitter, or just ice and add glitter to the area to be glittered first, then add everything else around it. Either way, the wetter the icing is, the more glitter will stick to it.

Baubles and sugar decorations: whenever you want to add ready-made decorations to your cookies, you need to either drop and gently press them onto wet icing or, if the area you want to add them to has already set, just squeeze on a tiny dot of line icing to use as a spot of "glue."

Writing: for fine details and writing, use line icing in your chosen color and make sure that you have either cut the tiniest tip off the piping bag for a fine line, or that you use a fine plain piping nozzle (No. 1). If you struggle to squeeze all the text or letters onto your cookie, try writing out the message or name to the correct scale on a computer, print it out, and then cover this with parchment paper to practice icing over the top. For larger cookies or individual letters, you can use flooding icing for thicker, smoother letters.

Dusts and shimmers: these are really fine edible glittery powders that can be rubbed or painted onto the iced cookie, a little like using makeup! They are used just on the surface and are really useful for adding a metallic sheen or pearlized look.

Icing a dot: hold the piping bag just above the surface where you want to make a little dot. Squeeze until you have the size of dot required, gently lifting as you go. Stop squeezing and then remove the piping bag.

Using nozzles: there is a large variety of piping nozzles and tubes in cookshops and cake-decorating shops. The different shapes create different icing trails as the icing is squeezed out. A star nozzle is great for little rosettes, and there are flat versions that are really useful for piping ribbons. Most of the effects that can be produced with a nozzle can be achieved with a disposable or paper piping bag, too. Cut across the end at an angle for icing trails with a flatter or oval-shaped profile. Cutting a tiny "v" instead of straight across produces a trail that is great for icing leaves. So buy a small selection of nozzles or experiment with cutting piping bags.

Making your own embellishments: if you have any leftover line icing, use it to make your own decorative embellishments. Pipe shapes onto parchment. Try little flowers or a lacy butterfly wing, initials or little animals. Either let them totally dry out naturally, or pop them into the drying oven for 30 minutes (see page 15). Finely detailed shapes are very fragile when dry and need to be peeled off carefully. If they are totally dry, these shapes can be kept for at least a month in an airtight container. You can use them to decorate cupcakes, too.

Plain Cookie Recipe

You can use this dough as a base for making all sorts of other flavors of cookies. Have a look at the following pages for some variations, as well as those listed below.

ingredients

makes 24 cookies

12oz / 3 cups all-purpose flour

4oz / 1 cup self-rising flour

4oz / ½ cup sugar

8 tablespoons salted butter, diced

½ cup corn syrup

1 large egg, lightly beaten

basic recipe

* Sift the flours together into a mixing bowl, add the sugar, and mix well.

* Add the butter. Using just the tips of your fingers, rub together the ingredients until the mixture resembles fine breadcrumbs.

* When all the butter is evenly mixed in, make a well in the center and add the syrup and the egg.

* Mix well, drawing in any of the flour left at the sides of the bowl and stop as soon as a ball has formed.

* Place the dough onto your clean work surface. Divide into two and squash the dough into two even-sized flat disks. Cover and chill until ready to use, or roll out immediately (see pages 18–19).

* For cutting, cooking, cooling, and keeping, follow the instructions on page 19.

variations on the theme

If there are some ingredients you want to experiment with, there are a couple of things to consider. If you are making dough for cookies that are to be rolled, cut and iced, then you don't want to add massive chunks of chocolate or hazelnut or whatever it is you have in mind, as they make the process quite tricky. So cut, break, or crunch up your ingredients into very small pieces before you use them. Add all dry ingredients to the flour and sugar and any liquid ingredients mixed in with the egg.

Nutmeg: add ½ tablespoon of grated nutmeg.

Ginger: add 1 tablespoon of ground ginger, and some finely diced crystallized ginger if you like.

Lemon: add the grated zest of two lemons.

Orange: add the grated zest of two oranges and little orange-flavored chocolate chunks.

Cinnamon and orange: add the grated zest of two oranges and ½ tablespoon of cinnamon.

Coffee: add 3 tablespoons of instant coffee dissolved in 1 tablespoon of water.

Cardamom: crush 8 dried cardamom pods and add the little dried seeds from inside the husks.

Super Chocolatey Cookies

This is a classic Biscuiteers' recipe. The cookies have a slightly doughy texture and the rich, bitter chocolateyness works beautifully with the sweet icing.

ingredients

makes 24 cookies

10oz / 2½ cups all-purpose flour

3.5oz / scant cup self-rising flour

2.5oz / ½ cup good-quality cocoa powder

4oz / ½ cup sugar

8 tablespoons salted butter, diced

½ cup corn syrup

1 large egg, lightly beaten

basic recipe

* Sift the flours and cocoa together into a mixing bowl, add the sugar and mix well.

* Add the butter. Using just the tips of your fingers, rub together the ingredients until the mixture resembles fine breadcrumbs.

* When all the butter is evenly mixed in, make a well in the center and add the syrup and the egg.

* Mix well, drawing in any of the flour left at the sides of the bowl and stop as soon as a ball has formed.

* Place the dough onto your clean work surface. Divide into two and squash the dough into two even-sized flat disks. Cover and chill until ready to use, or roll out immediately (see pages 18–19).

* For cutting, cooking, cooling, and keeping, follow the instructions on page 19.

variations on the theme

Orange: chocolate and orange is a time-honored flavor combination that works beautifully. Grate the zest of two medium oranges on the finest area of a grater. Stir the zest evenly into the beaten egg mixture and then follow the basic recipe. You can also add little chunks of orange-flavored chocolate to the mixture, too.

Vanilla Cookies

Natural vanilla has a delicious taste that is perfect for adding to cookies. At Biscuiteers we only use the whole pods of Madagascan vanilla for the finest flavor. You can also use good-quality natural vanilla essence or, at a pinch, vanilla flavoring.

ingredients

makes 24 cookies

½ vanilla pod or ½ teaspoon natural vanilla extract

12oz / 3 cups all-purpose flour

3.5oz / scant cup self-rising flour

4oz / ½ cup sugar

8 tablespoons salted butter, diced

½ cup corn syrup

1 large egg, lightly beaten

* If you are using the whole vanilla pod, slice down the pod with a sharp knife so that it splits in two. Scrape the tiny black seeds from the pod with a teaspoon and add to the sugar. If you are using vanilla extract, add to the lightly beaten egg.

* Sift the flours together into a mixing bowl, add the sugar and mix well.

* Add the butter. Using just the tips of your fingers, rub together the ingredients until the mixture resembles fine breadcrumbs.

* When all the butter is evenly mixed in, make a well in the center and add the syrup and the egg.

* Place the dough onto your clean work surface. Divide into two and squash the dough into two even-sized flat disks. Cover and chill until ready to use, or roll out immediately (see pages 18–19).

* For cutting, cooking, cooling, and keeping, follow the instructions on page 19.

Tip: you can pop the deseeded vanilla pod into a bag of sugar to make vanilla-scented sugar to use in your next batch of cookies.

Coconut Cookies

This recipe produces a delicate coconut-flavored cookie that has a slightly crunchier texture than the other recipes.

ingredients

makes 24 cookies

12oz / 3 cups all-purpose flour

3.5oz / scant cup self-rising flour

4 oz / ½ cup sugar

2.5oz / ¾ cup flaked coconut

8 tablespoons salted butter, diced

½ cup corn syrup

1 large egg, lightly beaten

* Sift the flours together into a mixing bowl, add the sugar and flaked coconut, and mix well.

* Add the butter. Using just the tips of your fingers, rub together the ingredients until the mixture resembles fine breadcrumbs.

* When all the butter is evenly mixed in, make a well in the center and add the syrup and the egg.

* Mix well, drawing in any of the flour left at the sides of the bowl, and stop as soon as a ball has formed.

* Place the dough onto your clean worktop. Divide into two and squash the dough into two even-sized flat disks. Cover and chill until ready to use, or roll out immediately (see pages 18–19).

* For cutting, cooking, cooling, and keeping, follow the instructions on page 19.

Simple Butter Cookies

These lovely shortbread-style cookies have a satisfying buttery taste and are really good for the Bake with Mother collection (see pages 136–139). They are slightly more fragile and crumbly than the other cookies, so they're not ideal if you have to transport them very far.

ingredients

makes approx. 30 cookies

18oz / 4½ cups all-purpose flour

6oz / ¾ cup sugar

1 cup (2 sticks) salted butter, diced

2 large eggs, lightly beaten

splash of milk, if required

* Sift the flour and sugar together into a mixing bowl and mix well.

* Add the butter. Using just the tips of your fingers, rub together the ingredients until the mixture resembles fine breadcrumbs.

* When all the butter is evenly mixed in, make a well in the center and add the eggs and a splash of milk, if required, to bring it all together into a smooth dough.

* Place the dough onto your clean work surface. Divide into two and squash the dough into two even-sized flat disks. Cover and chill until ready to use, or roll out immediately (see pages 18–19).

* For cutting, cooking, cooling, and keeping, follow the instructions on page 19.

Almond / Hazelnut Cookies

These cookies are lovely served alongside fruity desserts. Their delicate nutty flavor makes them great to enjoy un-iced, too.

ingredients

makes 24 cookies

12oz / 3 cups all-purpose flour

4oz / ½ cup sugar

8 tablespoons salted butter, diced

3.5oz / 1 cup ground almonds or 1 teaspoon of almond extract or ¾ cup toasted hazelnuts, chopped

½ cup corn syrup

1 large egg, lightly beaten

* Sift the flour into a mixing bowl, add the sugar, and mix well.

* Add the butter. Using just the tips of your fingers, rub together the ingredients until the mixture resembles fine breadcrumbs.

* When all the butter is evenly mixed in, add the almonds or hazelnuts and stir in evenly.

* Make a well in the center and add the syrup and the egg, and the almond extract if using.

* Mix well, drawing in any of the flour left at the side of the bowl, and stop as soon as a ball has formed.

* Place the dough onto your clean worktop. Divide into two and squash the dough into two even-sized flat disks. Cover and chill until ready to use, or roll out immediately (see pages 18–19).

* For cutting, cooking, cooling, and keeping, follow the instructions on page 19.

Gluten-free Chocolate Cookies

The texture of these cookies is certainly more shortbready than our usual cookie recipes. These cookies need to be fully dried as their crumbly texture makes them liable to get a little soft when the icing is piped on. You also need to ensure that the icing colors and ingredients are gluten-free.

ingredients

makes 24 cookies

9oz gluten-free flour (cup measure depends on the type of flour)

pinch salt

3.5oz / scant cup sugar

7 tablespoons butter

14oz dark chocolate

* Sift all the dry ingredients into a bowl and mix together.

* Melt the butter and chocolate together carefully over a low heat and pour into the dry ingredients.

* Stir well, and then using just the tips of your fingers, rub together the ingredients until the mixture comes together. Stop as soon as a ball can be formed.

* Place the dough onto your clean work surface. Divide into two and squash the dough into two even-sized flat disks. Cover and chill until ready to use, or roll out immediately (see pages 18–19).

* For cutting, cooking, cooling, and keeping, follow the instructions on page 19.

Anzac Cookies

These Australian classics have a mixture of oats and coconut to thank for their lovely crunchy texture. Dry them out carefully when they have been iced to keep their delicate, crumbly texture.

ingredients

makes 24 cookies

9oz / 2 cups all-purpose flour

½ teaspoon baking powder

2½ cups steel-cut oats

1⅓ cups flaked coconut

5oz / ⅔ cup sugar

12 tablespoons butter, diced

1 tablespoon corn syrup

1 large egg, lightly beaten

* Sift the flour and baking powder together into a mixing bowl.

* Stir in the coconut, oats, and sugar.

* Add the butter. Using just the tips of your fingers, rub together the ingredients until the mixture resembles fine breadcrumbs.

* When all the butter is evenly mixed in, make a well in the center and add the syrup and the egg.

* Mix well, drawing in any of the flour left at the sides of the bowl, and stop as soon as a ball has formed.

* Place the dough onto your clean work surface. Divide into two and squash the dough into two even-sized flat disks. Cover and chill until ready to use, or roll out immediately (see pages 18–19).

* For cutting, cooking, cooling, and keeping, follow the instructions on page 19.

Peanut Butter Cookies

We love the savory flavor that the peanuts bring to this recipe. You can use crunchy or smooth peanut butter, depending on what is in your pantry, though the crunchy one does have a lovely texture.

ingredients

makes 24 cookies

9oz / 2 cups all-purpose flour

3.5oz / ½ cup brown sugar

½ teaspoon baking powder

4 tablespoons butter, diced

1 egg, lightly beaten

¼ cup corn syrup

1–2 tablespoons milk

¼ cup peanut butter

* Sift the flour, sugar, and baking powder into a mixing bowl and mix well.

* Add the butter. Using just the tips of your fingers, rub together the ingredients until the mixture resembles fine breadcrumbs.

* In a separate bowl, mix together the egg, syrup, one tablespoon of milk, and the peanut butter.

* Make a well in the center of the dry ingredients and add the liquid mixture. Bring it all together to form a soft dough. Add a dash more milk if required.

* Place the dough onto your clean work surface. Divide into two and squash the dough into two even sized flat disks. Cover and chill until ready to use, or roll out immediately (see pages 18–19).

* For cutting, cooking, cooling, and keeping, follow the instructions on page 19.

Molasses Spice Cookies

This is a lovely recipe that is perfect for making ornament-shaped cookies to hang on the Christmas tree or gingerbread men.

ingredients

makes 24 cookies

7oz / scant cup all-purpose flour

½ teaspoon baking powder

½ teaspoon ground ginger

½ teaspoon cinnamon

½ teaspoon pumpkin pie spice

2 tablespoons dark brown sugar

7 tablespoons salted butter, diced

¼ cup molasses

* Sift the flour, baking powder, and all the spices into a mixing bowl. Add the sugar and mix well.

* Add the butter. Using just the tips of your fingers, rub together the ingredients until the mixture resembles fine breadcrumbs.

* When all the butter is evenly mixed in, make a well in the center and add the molasses and bring it all together. You will know when it is all mixed in as it will have an even color all over with not too many streaks of molasses.

* Place the dough onto your clean work surface. Divide into two and squash the dough into two even-sized flat disks. Cover and chill until ready to use, or roll out immediately (see pages 18–19).

* For cooking, cooling, and keeping, follow the instructions on page 19.

Festive
&
Seasonal

Traditional Advent

This collection is just one more excuse to ice some cookies at Christmas. Have a look at all the traditional Christmas images that you can find and use them as inspiration for your twenty-four advent cookies. Add sparkles and glitter, snowflakes and tiny shiny baubles, gold leaf or shimmering dust. Hide each cookie in a tiny stocking, wrap them in squares of festive paper, or sew yourself a keepsake calendar like the one here.

Iced Christmas

Everyone loves this sparkling Christmas collection. Simple and jolly, this has appeal for the whole family. White gift-tag cookies iced with Christmas messages and the names of your nearest and dearest make great place settings on Christmas day, too.

cutters

tree
reindeer (see page 148)
snowflake
snowman
stocking
sleigh

recipes

1 quantity cinnamon-and-orange-flavored Plain Cookie dough (see page 33); makes 2 stockings, 3 reindeer, 1 sleigh, 2 snowmen, and 1 large Christmas tree

1 quantity Basic Royal Icing (see page 21)

line icing

donkey brown
forest green
white
black
red

flooding icing

white
baby blue

embellishments

silver and gold baubles
silver sparkly glitter sugar

Christmas tree

Ice the trunk with donkey brown line icing. * Use forest green line icing to add boughs. Start at the top and work down to base. Allow to dry for at least 5 minutes. * Use white runny icing to add "snow" on the tips of all the branches and sprinkle with silver glitter before it dries. * Drop on tiny silver and gold baubles and any other embellishments you want to add.

Rudolph and friends

Carefully outline head, body, and legs in white. Allow to dry for at least 5 minutes. * Flood with white. Allow to dry. * Add ears in white, eye in black, and red nose. * Ice antlers in fine donkey brown line and a bow if you wish in any color.

snowflake

Pipe the outline in white and leave to dry. * Flood with white runny icing and, when dry, use more white line and glitter if you wish to add flake details.

snowman

Ice the hat using black line icing. * Use white line icing to outline head and body. Allow to dry for at least 5 minutes. * Flood with white. Pop all the little air bubbles that form with a toothpick if you want a perfect finish. Allow to dry. * Pipe on the scarf in the color of your choice. Finish with a little red radish nose, eyes, and some black buttons. * You could also add a sprig of holly or a robin to the hat.

stocking

Outline in white and allow to dry for at least 5 minutes. * Flood the middle with white and allow to dry until totally set. * Ice on little spots where you want glitter. Sprinkle on glitter and carefully shake off excess. * Make outline for presents in any color, allow to dry, and fill with flooding icing. Allow to dry. * Pipe on ribbons and bows and your chosen pattern on the stocking.

sleigh

Outline the sleigh in red line. Allow to dry for at least 5 minutes. * Flood with baby blue flooding icing. Allow to dry until totally set. * Ice on little spots of white where you want frosting to be. Sprinkle on silver glitter before spots dry; carefully shake off excess. * Add runners and swirls in red line.

Christmas Ornaments

Making cookies at Christmas time is great: you can give them as presents, use them as decoration, advent treats, or even as place names on the Christmas table. These ornaments are specially designed to hang on your tree, and they each have a little hole at the top to thread through with pretty ribbon. They can even be iced on both sides: just let the first side dry totally before icing on the reverse.

kit

ornament cutters, or you can just use some basic round and fluted cutters in different sizes wide drinking straws pretty ribbon or thread

recipes

1 quantity cinnamon-and-orange flavored Plain Cookie dough (see page 33) or Molasses Spice Cookies dough (see page 39). Aim to make ¾ of each ornament

1 quantity Basic Royal Icing (see page 21)

line icing

parma violet
baby pink
fuchsia
lime green
forest green

flooding icing

red
white
baby pink
fuchsia

embellishments

gold and silver balls
sugar snowflakes
glitter sugar in pink

Helpful hints: roll and cut your cookies as per the dough instructions, but remember to cut a hole at the top of each cookie with the end of a drinking straw BEFORE baking. Remember to ice AROUND each hole so you can easily thread through with ribbon.

trellis ornament

Outline the bauble in parma violet line. Add pink line tassel and fuchsia detail around the ribbon hole. * When dry, flood the circle with red and wait for a minute to let it set. * Pipe the crisscross pattern in parma violet line. * Add the dots of lime green icing and the little golden balls to decorate.

teardrop ornament

This is all iced in line icing. * Use your own favorite colors. * Separating each band with a forest green stripe, ice all the way down in colored bands. * Drop gold and silver balls onto the decoration while the icing is still wet.

candy cane

Pipe around the outline and the hole in pink line and allow to dry. * Flood with white runny icing, remove air bubbles with a toothpick, and leave to set. * Ice the candy stripes in alternate baby pink and lime green lines.

spinning top ornament

Outline the bauble in lime green line icing. Flood the middle with baby pink runny icing and allow to set. * Pipe around the ribbon hole in fuchsia and then add the lines of lime green across the bauble. * Add zigzag detail in forest green and use fuchsia for the little polka dots.

swedish sweater ornament

Ice outline in lime green line icing and pipe red around the ribbon hole. * Flood the middle with fuchsia flooding icing and allow to set. * Add lime green and forest green for the zigzags and polka dots. * Drop sugar snowflakes onto the icing while it is still wet.

Christmas Tree

This cookie "tree" is very simple but it looks impressive. It is made up of a stack of little Christmas stars, which can be decorated and detailed or kept plain and simply dusted with confectioners' sugar. This is a great treat to make with children. It is a good idea to make this tree close to where you are going to eat it.

cutters

up to 6 different-sized
5-pointed stars

recipes

1 quantity Molasses Spice
Cookies dough (see page 39)
or cinnamon-and-orange
flavored Plain Cookie dough
(see page 33); makes approx.
30 cookies

½ quantity Basic Royal Icing
(see page 21)

line icing

white for decorating
and "gluing"

Note: colored line icing
required if you're going to
opt for colorful decoration

embellishments

(optional)
confectioners' sugar
glitter sugar
shiny baubles
snowflakes

Cut about five or six cookies in each star size and bake as usual. To ice, add a white line around the edge of each star and dust with silver glitter. Add a silver bauble to each star point using white line icing as glue. Allow to dry.

Take a pretty plate and, starting with the largest stars, stack them on top of each other using white line icing to "glue" each layer together. Give each additional star a quarter turn to make the helix shape.

Allow to dry completely about halfway through so you have a stable platform on which to stack the smaller stars.

decorating ideas

Simple: sift confectioners' sugar over the entire tree to make it look like a frosted fir.

Colorful: squeeze trails of multi-colored line icing all over the tree. Add glitter sugar and tiny shiny baubles, snowflakes, or any other exciting Christmas decorations to the trails before they set.

Sophisticated: ice each star with a glitter-frosted white pattern and stack up with pretty candies. Add small iced decorations like those used on the Wedding Cake on pages 78–81. You can make baubles and candy canes, little robins and holly sprigs, candles, and gingerbread men.

Easter Eggs

Fabergé darling? We have taken our inspiration for our largest eggs from Fabergé's most precious of Easter offerings. Eggs of Easter past have influenced our other patterns that are full of pretty spots, dots, and braids. Make up your own designs, in your favorite colors, or ice the smallest ovals like little speckled songbird eggs.

cutters

3 different-sized egg cutters

recipes

1 quantity Super Chocolately Cookies dough (see page 34); makes 5 large, 7 medium, and 10 small eggs

1 quantity Basic Royal Icing (see page 21)

line icing

fuchsia
pea green
Aegean blue
white

flooding icing

baby pink
baby blue
fuchsia

embellishments

gold and silver glitter sugar
gold and silver baubles

Fabergé sparkler

Pipe outline of the largest egg in fuchsia and dry for 5 minutes. * Flood with baby pink runny icing and allow to dry. * When set add the jewel outline, all the swirls, dots, and lines that you want to make your pattern in pea green line. * When everything is totally dry, flood the center of the jewel in baby blue flooding icing and sprinkle with silver glitter sugar.
* Finally add any glittering baubles using line icing as glue.

all wrapped up egg

Pipe outline of the smallest egg in fuchsia and dry for 5 minutes. * Flood with baby pink flooding icing and allow to dry. * Use your favorite colors of line icing (we use Aegean blue, pea green, white, and fuchsia here) to add spots, rick-rack, that old-fashioned wavy ribbon, and lines for the perfect pretty pattern.

dotty egg

Outline the egg in fuchsia line and leave to dry for five minutes.
* Just fill the center of the egg with flooding fuchsia icing (don't overfill or it will overflow when the dots are added) and immediately add spots of flooding icing to make the dotty pattern, before the icing has had a chance to set.

Tips: if you would like to use your beautiful bejeweled cookies to decorate an Easter tree, cut a hole with the end of a drinking straw in the top of each egg before you bake the cookies. Thread pretty ribbon through the hole after the cookies have been iced and dried.

Joys of Spring

We love the kissing bunnies and the little lambs and the all-round freshness of this sweet springtime collection. There are a whole host of suitable cutters available—you'll be spoiled for choice!

cutters

lamb
bunny (see page 150)
egg
chick
primroses

recipes

1 quantity Super Chocolately Cookies dough (see page 31); make around 20 if you make lots of little eggs, too

1 quantity Basic Royal Icing (see page 21)

line icing

black
white
baby pink
baby blue
donkey brown
bright yellow
primrose

flooding icing

Aegean blue
white
donkey brown
bright yellow
primrose

lamb

Use either black or white line icing to ice fluffy balls of wool all over. Allow to dry for 5 minutes. * Add eyes in black and a nose in baby pink.

bunny

Use whichever color you like to outline the bunny shape. * Allow to dry for 5 minutes and then flood the entire bunny in runny icing of the same color. * When this has set, add a fluffy tail and ear details in white line. * Add a ribbon in a contrasting line color and, finally, add the eye with a tiny spot of black line and baby pink for the nose.

egg

Ice the outline first in either baby blue or donkey brown line. Allow to dry for 5 minutes. * Flood with Aegean blue or donkey brown and immediately add a few contrasting blue or brown dots. * Muddle them into the background to create a speckled effect using the tip of a toothpick.

chick

Outline chick in yellow line. Allow to dry for 5 minutes. * Flood with yellow. Allow to dry. * Add wing and feather details in yellow line. * Add a beak in baby pink line and an eye in black.

primroses

Use a primrose yellow line to pipe outline around flowers. Allow to dry for 5 minutes. * Flood the flower with primrose yellow. Allow to dry. * Pipe bright yellow centers in the flowers.

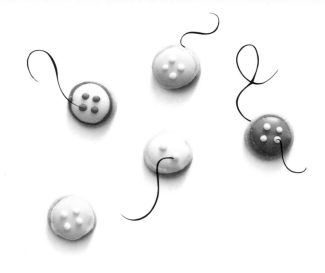

Mother's Day

This is the sewing basket that no mother should be without as it is packed with all the essentials. Find a little basket and line it with pretty material or tissue paper and place the cookies inside. A lovely gift for Mom.

cutters

rectangles for needles
spools of thread (see page 147)
large round cutter for
balls of wool
thimble
scissors (see page 147)
tiny round cutter for buttons
strawberry pincushion (see
page 147)

recipes

1 quantity Molasses Spice
Cookies dough (see page 39);
makes approx. 19 cookies

1 quantity Basic Royal Icing
(see page 21)

line icing

white
baby pink
primrose
red
ivory
Aegean blue
forest green

flooding icing

baby blue
white
ivory
red

needles

Ice a scalloped outline in white and allow to dry for about 5 minutes. * Fill with baby blue flooding icing and allow to set. * Use line icing to add flower pattern * Add the needles in white and thread in red.

spools of thread

Pipe the thread on spool in line icing of your choice. * Add outline of wooden spool in white line and allow to dry for 5 minutes. * Flood this area with white and allow to set. * Add details to spool in any color line icing.

balls of wool

Using just line icing, in any color, pipe on fine lines in the pattern of a ball of wool.

thimble

Using line icing, pipe on the pattern of the thimble.

scissors

Ice handles in ivory outline. * Use Aegean blue to outline the blades and allow to dry for 5 minutes. * Flood the blades with white and the handles in ivory and allow to set. * Add details to blades with Aegean blue line icing.

buttons

Ice around the outline and the holes in your chosen line color and allow to dry for 5 minutes. * Flood with a different color and allow to set. * Add any details to the buttons with line icing.

strawberry pincushion

Ice little leaves and stalk on top of the strawberry in forest green line. * Ice strawberry in red line in a wiggly "knitted" pattern, and add flowers and ribbon in line icing too. Allow to dry. * Pipe little white pins and finish off with dots of color on the ends.

Father's Day

This is one set of tools that Dad will really enjoy getting out. You can make this collection as elaborate or simple as you like. Add some power tools and goggles or just make lots of paintbrushes with different "paint" on the ends.

cutters

pliers
saw
paintbrush (see page 149)
hammer
screwdriver
wrench
wire cutters

recipes

Use your father's favorite cookie dough

1 quantity Basic Royal Icing (see page 21)

line icing

red
gray
bright yellow
black
add more colors for different paints on the brushes if you like

flooding icing

red
gray
bright yellow
black

pliers

Pipe the outline of handles in red line and the jaws of the pliers in gray. Remember to leave a little hole. Allow to dry for 5 minutes. * Flood handles in red and jaws in gray. * Add detail with gray line.

saw

Outline handle in yellow line and the blade in gray. Allow to dry for 5 minutes. * Flood the handle with yellow and the blade with gray.

paintbrush

Outline the handle in yellow line and the part that holds the bristles in gray. Allow to dry. * Flood the handle with yellow and the bristle holder with gray. * Pipe the bristles in black line. Allow to dry. * Using flooding icing, carefully squeeze the "paint" onto the bristles.

hammer

Pipe around head of the hammer with gray line. Outline the handle in black. Allow to dry for 5 minutes. * Flood the handle with black and the head with gray. Allow to dry. * Add stripe detail in red line on the handle.

screwdriver

Outline the handle in yellow line and the screwdriver in gray. Allow to dry for 5 minutes. * Flood the handle with yellow and the screwdriver with gray. * Add the handle detail in black line.

wrenches and wire cutters

Ice around the outline in gray line. Allow to dry for 5 minutes. * Flood with gray icing. * Add details in black line if you wish.

Witch's Spell

We love the idea of spells and cauldrons so here are all the ingredients for a truly terrifying witches' brew, to be cast under the watchful eyes of the owl and the black cat. Spells still work just as well with only a couple of ingredients, so choose your favorites from our collection.

cutters

pumpkin
ghost
bat
snake
newt
witch
cat
mouse

recipes

1 quantity Molasses Spice Cookies dough (see page 39); makes at least 16, add more snakes and mice to use up any spare dough

1 quantity Basic Royal Icing (see page 21)

line icing

green
orange
white
black
bright yellow
donkey brown
gray

flooding icing

orange
white
black
forest green
gray

embellishments

silver and red glitter

pumpkin

Use green line to make stalk detail. Pipe orange line around edge of pumpkin and add eye and mouth details. Allow to dry for 5 minutes. * Flood with orange. Allow to dry. * Add orange lines for stripes to finish, if wished.

little ghost

Outline the body of ghost in white. Outline the eyes and mouth in orange. Allow to dry for 5 minutes. * Flood with white runny icing and allow to dry.

big bat

Ice around wing outline in black and pipe a little oval line for the tummy. Allow to dry for 5 minutes. * Flood the wings and head with black. After 1 minute, sprinkle on silver glitter and flood the tummy with black. Allow to dry. * Brush off excess glitter and add two yellow eyes.

snake

Outline in green. Allow to dry for 5 minutes. * Flood with green. Before it has a chance to set, pipe on tiny yellow spots. Allow to dry. * Pipe on nose and eye details.

newt

Ice around outline of body in green line and add little feet. Allow to dry. * Flood body in green and pipe on tiny yellow or orange spots before green icing sets. * Add little white eyes with black pupils.

witch

Ice around witch's cloak, hair, and hat in black and face in green line. Allow to dry for 5 minutes. * Flood entire witch's cloak, hair, and hat in black and allow to dry. * Pipe broom with brown line and add stockings in striped line and dry. * Pipe little orange shoes and cover in sparkling red glitter.

cat

Outline in black line. Allow to dry for 5 minutes. * Flood the center with black and allow to dry. * Add a bright yellow collar and black and orange eye.

Note: some black colors stain mouths and teeth; settle for a charcoal gray if you don't want black fangs.

mini mouse

Outline the body of mouse in gray. Allow to dry for 5 minutes. * Flood with gray. Allow to dry. * Use fine black line to add eye, nose, and ear details and little paws.

Chanukah

This is a very simple-to-ice collection in celebration of Chanukah. We have used the traditional color palette to ice all the shapes. We think that you might find these cookies go down very well at any one of the eight festival nights. Take some of the cookie ideas to use as favors at bar mitzvahs or bat mitzvahs, too.

cutters

Star of David
dreidel
menorah
rectangle (for gifts)

recipes

1 quantity lemon flavored Plain Cookie dough (see page 33); makes approx. 15 cookies

1 quantity Basic Royal Icing (see page 21)

line icing

gentian blue
white
bright yellow (tiny amount)
baby blue

flooding icing

gentian blue
white
baby blue

embellishments

silver glitter

Star of David and dreidel

Ice the outline and flood all in white. * Dry and then add details in gentian line. Add silver glitter before the line dries if you wish.

Menorah

Outline and flood in gentian blue and leave to set. * Ice on the candles in white and finish with yellow line-icing flames.

polka dot gift

Pipe the outline in gentian blue line icing and leave to set. * Flood until just full with white runny icing and then immediately squeeze on spots of gentian blue runny icing. * Leave to set, then add the ribbon and bow detail in gentian blue line.

star gift

Pipe on outline of the shape of the gift in baby blue. * Leave to set and then flood with gentian blue, white, or baby blue runny icing. When dry, pipe on the ribbon and bow details in contrasting line icing.

little present

Ice smaller versions of the presents detailed above.

Thanksgiving

This is the Biscuiteers' homage to all good things at Thanksgiving. You can ice similar selections to celebrate harvest, too.

cutters

pumpkin
leaves (see page 153)
turkey
acorn (see page 153)
apple (see page 153)

recipes

1 quantity cinnamon-and-orange-flavored Plain Cookie dough (see page 33); makes at least 20 if you use small leaf cutters

1 quantity Basic Royal Icing (see page 21)

line icing

pea green
orange
donkey brown
red
eucalyptus

flooding icing

orange
eucalyptus
red

pumpkin

Use pea green line to add stalk detail at top. * Pipe orange line all around edge. Allow to dry for 5 minutes. * Flood with orange icing. Allow to set. * Add orange lines for the stripes on pumpkin.

leaves

All leaves are iced in same way. Outline in a line color of your choice and allow to dry for 5 minutes. * Flood in the same color. Don't make it too full if you want to add spots and colors. Add these before the first layer sets. Allow to dry. * Ice on vein details.

turkey

Use line icing to pipe feathers and details on turkey. Start at beak and gradually add feathers all way down in brown, orange, red, and eucalyptus. * Add little donkey brown feet, too.

acorn

Ice cup with donkey brown line crisscross pattern. Outline around acorn in eucalyptus. Allow to dry for 5 minutes. * Flood acorn with same eucalyptus icing.

apple

Pipe around outline of apple in red. Add stalk in brown and leaf in pea green line. Allow to dry for 5 minutes. * Flood apple with red runny icing.

I Love You Madly

This simple-to-ice collection of cookies has been designed to make messy icing look good. They are perfect to have some fun with and send a romantic message at the same time. Write "I LOVE YOU"— in a mad fashion... and you don't have to wait for Valentine's Day!

cutters

letters (in any size you like)
hearts

recipes

1 quantity lemon flavored Plain Cookie dough (see page 33); makes approx. 16 cookies

1 quantity Basic Royal Icing (see page 21)

line icing

eucalyptus
hydrangea
rose
raspberry
pea green
primrose
Aegean blue

embellishments

colored baubles

the instructions are simple...

Squeeze squiggles of line icing all over the letters and hearts just like wiggly spaghetti. * Vary the order in which you add the colors if you like and add little baubles if you want some sparkle. For a more sophisticated look, ice an outline, flood, and dry before icing madly.

Valentine's Love Hearts

These vintage-inspired hearts with their simple roses and polka dots are easy to make your mark on. Write your love large across them if you wish. Add a simple question mark, initials, or even a "Will you marry me?" Just make sure that whomever you give them to is worthy of such a beautiful collection of cookies.

cutters

hearts

recipes

1 quantity Super Chocolatey Cookies dough (see page 34); cut all the hearts you desire

1 quantity Basic Royal Icing (see page 21)

line icing

white
lime green
baby pink
raspberry

flooding icing

baby pink
white

Pipe an outline just inside each heart. Allow to dry for 5 minutes. * Flood the centers. For a perfect finish you may need to burst the little air bubbles that appear under the surface of the flooding icing with the tip of a toothpick. Do this before the icing has a chance to set. * If you want to add stripes or polka dots in flooding icing, do not overfill the centers and add your design while the icing is still wet. For smaller hearts, plain flooding or just tiny polka dot decorations work best. * Allow centers to dry before adding roses, ribbons, leaves, or polka dots in line icing. * Ice little lacy ruffles around the outsides of the hearts.

Tips: If you want to add a written message, practice on parchment paper with your message written or printed underneath so you know exactly what size and style of lettering will fit on your heart.

If you want to send one of these cookies instead of a Valentine's card, have a look at our Packaging ideas on pages 140–142 to make sure that it will be one heart that definitely doesn't get broken on Valentine's Day.

Special Occasions

New Baby

This is the sweetest little collection to celebrate a new baby. Think light pastel shades when it comes to mixing your colors, and don't feel that you have to do all three different shades. A row of little ducks all one color looks just as good, and they are all delightfully simple to ice, too. Make the line icing a couple of shades darker than the flooding icing.

cutters

mommy and baby duck
(see page 150)

recipes

1 quantity Simple Butter
Cookies dough (see page 37)
or Vanilla Cookies dough
(see page 36) if mailing;
makes 6 mommy ducks
and 18 baby ducks

1 quantity Basic Royal Icing
(see page 21)

line icing

bright yellow
baby pink
baby blue
primrose
black (tiny amount)

flooding icing

baby pink
baby blue
primrose

All of the ducks are decorated
in the same way.

Pipe on the beak with bright yellow line
icing, then outline around the entire
edge of the cookies in either baby pink,
baby blue, or primrose yellow. Allow to
dry for about 5 minutes. * Fill in the head
and body area with the flooding icing
that matches your chosen line color.
* If any air bubbles appear, pop them
with the tip of a toothpick and gently tap
the cookie to even out the surface. Allow
to set completely. * Ice on a ribbon and
bow at the neck using line icing and then
use black to make a little spot for the eye.

Baby Shower

This is such a sweet collection, and it is beautifully simple to ice. We have used primrose yellow for all of the trimmings, but you can change that for baby pink or powder blue icing if you know what is expected!

cutters

rattle
carriage
bootie
teddy bear (see page 151)
block
baby onesie

recipes

1 quantity of Vanilla Cookies dough (see page 36); aim to make 24 cookies

1 quantity Basic Royal Icing (see page 21)

line icing

white
primrose
donkey brown

flooding icing

white
teddy brown

rattle

Pipe outline in white line and leave to dry. * Fill with white flooding icing. Remove air bubbles by pricking them with the tip of a toothpick. * Allow to dry briefly and then add little details in primrose line.

carriage

Ice the wheel and spokes in brown line icing and the outline of the hood and carriage in white. * Allow to dry and then flood with white runny icing. * Remove air bubbles by pricking them with the tip of a toothpick. * When set, add details in primrose line icing to the hood and the sides of the carriage. * Finish with a little lacy ruffle to the front of the hood in white line icing.

bootie

Ice on the knitted pattern just as with the onesie, remembering to change the direction of icing to make the heel and toe. * Allow to set, then add the ribbon using primrose line.

teddy bear

Pipe outline of head, arms, legs, feet, muzzle, and ears in brown line icing. * Leave to set then flood feet and muzzle with white and the rest of the body in brown runny icing. * Finally pipe the details of nose, eyes, and ears in brown line.

block

Ice all around the outside with primrose line. * Flood with white runny icing. * Allow to dry briefly, then add cube details and ABC with primrose.

baby onesie

Using white line icing, pipe on "knitted" texture to the entire onesie. * Let this set, then add seam details and snaps in yellow line.

Birthday

This is a traditional birthday collection celebrating the simple pleasures of the special day. Easy to cut and easy to ice, you can personalize it with your own messages and write the recipient's name and address on the envelope if you like, too. Add variety by icing the wrapping paper on the presents in lots of different lovely designs.

cutters

cake (see page 148)
envelope
present (see page 148, or cut by hand)

recipes

1 quantity lemon flavored Plain Cookie dough (see page 33); makes at least 16

1 quantity Basic Royal Icing (see page 21)

line icing

baby pink
hydrangea
raspberry
pea green
white
bright yellow
red

flooding icing

baby pink
hydrangea
gentian blue
pea green

embellishments

sparkly glitter
shiny baubles
(if the recipient likes a bit of sparkle!)

cake

Outline all three layers of cake in baby pink line icing. Allow to dry for 5 minutes. * Flood with pink. Leave until surface has set. * Add ribbons in hydrangea, raspberry, and pea green line icing. * Ice candles in white line, and add little yellow flames.

envelope

Ice around the outline in hydrangea line and allow to dry for 5 minutes. * Flood with hydrangea and, before it sets, add the details in pea green line icing.

presents

Decorate the presents in a variety of patterns. Look at the icing patterns on pages 29–31 to choose your favorite. * Ice around present in line icing. Allow to set for 5 minutes. * Flood with your favorite color and follow instructions for pattern—polka dots, plain, stripes, spots, initials, etc. Don't overfill with flooding icing if you are going to add lots of detail—it will spill over icing walls. * Allow to set. * Add ribbons, bows, etc. in line icing.

Home Sweet Home

These houses are great to ice. We have chosen a tiny village's worth here, but the possibilities are endless. They make a lovely housewarming or "welcome home" gift and you can add your own and friends' houses to the collection, too. Ice roses over the doors, geraniums in pots, pets peeping out of the windows, and whatever little details turn them from houses into homes.

cutters

square
rectangle
(or cut freehand with a knife)

recipes

1 quantity Vanilla Cookies dough (see page 36); number made depends on how big you want your houses to be

1 quantity Basic Royal Icing (see page 21)

line icing

white
donkey brown
gray
raspberry
black
fuchsia
red

flooding icing

white
baby blue
gray
teddy brown
lime green

thatched cottage

Ice door and window outlines in white line icing. * Add thatch in brown line. * Outline cottage in white and allow to dry. * Flood with white. * Use line icing to add timber frame, chimney, and door details and any other decorations.

fisherman's cottage

Pipe outline of slate roof in gray line. Add windows, wall lines, and door details in white line and allow to dry. * Flood house in baby blue and roof in gray. Allow to set. * Add details in line icing for windows, house name, and cat (not pictured).

front door

Choose whichever colors you like. Outline whole door in colored line and leave to dry. * Flood with chosen color and allow to set. * Pipe on door panels, knocker, and handle details in line icing.

town house

Pipe a white outline around windows and the blue wall area. Allow to dry. * Flood in baby blue. * When set, add details to windows in white line, and roof and door in raspberry line.

castle

Ice the outline of the turrets, walls, doors, and windows in brown line and allow to dry. * Flood all of the stonework with gray or teddy brown runny icing. Allow to set. * Use line icing to add the stone, stairs, and brick details. * Add the doors and final details in black line.

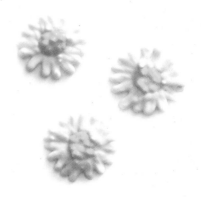

Cake Decorations

equipment

parchment paper
nozzles
piping bags

recipes

1 quantity Basic Royal Icing
(see page 21)

line icing

choose your
favorite colors

flooding icing

choose your
favorite colors

embellishments

a little light glitter

There is more to baking than just cookies. However, we find that the softer and more uneven texture of cakes makes icing the Biscuiteers way a little tricky. We make our own decorations by icing onto parchment or parchment/silicone sheets, allowing them to dry, and then adding these to the top of cupcakes or birthday and wedding cakes.

If you are using parchment, you can trace over your favorite designs with the icing. Whatever you choose to do, make sure that the lines are not too delicate as they will break on removal from the parchment, and that the little decorations are placed into a warm oven at the lowest heat setting and totally dried before being peeled off the backing.

Any of our cookie designs can be iced onto parchment. Take the sheets of parchment

or silicone and place them on a baking sheet. Start with the outlines and ice in the normal way until you have as many decorations as you need. Little iced shapes are lovely for children's individual cakes. Try bumblebees, butterflies, ladybugs, and flowers for pretty cakes. Or snails, snakes, lizards, beetles, and frogs for more robust little Biscuiteers. When the shapes are all totally dry and have been peeled off the parchment paper, you can use them like the store-bought decorations. They will keep for several weeks in an airtight container as long as they are totally dry before being packed up. Layer them up between sheets of wax paper to protect them and keep them from breaking.

You can make or buy cakes to decorate. Use buttercream frosting as a base and press the decorations into this, or use line icing as "glue" to stick the little shapes onto the sides and top of more formal cakes. Keep it simple…or go as wild as you like.

Bridal Collection

Ice these cookies for your friends' weddings, give them as gifts to the flower girls, or bake in celebration of an engagement. We have chosen ivory as our background color, but for ease of icing and mixing, you can simply ice the whole collection in white.

cutters

There are lots of cookie cutters available with a wedding theme. Share the love with loads of little hearts and have a go at designing your own wedding dress.

recipes

1 quantity Vanilla Cookies dough (see page 36); makes at least 16 larger cookies and heaps of little hearts cut from any trimmings

1 quantity Basic Royal Icing (see page 21)

line icing

ivory
gentian blue
baby pink
parma violet
lime green

flooding icing

ivory
gentian blue
baby pink

embellishments

Add a few subtle sparkles or a cascade of crystals and anything in between.

dress

Design your own fantastic creation. From massive meringue to sleek sparkling gown, this is one cookie that you can totally go to town on. * Ice your outline and allow it to set, flood with runny icing, remove bubbles, and allow to set. * Add details over the top in line icing. Allow to dry totally, then use line icing as a "glue" to stick on glitter or baubles where you want them.

shoes

Make yours a copy of the bride's or ice one of the many shoe shapes available. Outline the shoe shape in ivory and allow to set for 5 minutes. * Flood with runny ivory icing and allow to set briefly before adding sparkles, glitter, or baubles, or allow to set fully and ice on more details of bows and flowers in colored line.

love hearts

Ice the outline in line icing and allow to set for 5 minutes, then flood with runny icing. Use gentian blue, pink, and ivory colors.

dove

Ice the outline in ivory and set for 5 minutes. * Flood with ivory runny icing, remove any air bubbles, then allow to dry. * Add the wing and eye detail in ivory.

wedding cake

Ice the outlines in ivory line and allow to dry for 5 minutes. * Flood with ivory runny icing, remove any air bubbles, and then allow to set. * Ice on the swags and bows and any initials or names in ivory line icing.

bunch of flowers

We have chosen pastel colors for our collection, but the flowers can be iced in bright and beautiful colors, too. The whole bunch is iced using outline icing only. * Start with lime green stalks, then add the flowers in all the colors and some leaves in between. * Finally, add a bow to the stems.

Wedding Favors

From little organza bags filled with pastel-colored hearts, to place card cookies with wedding guest names, there are so many reasons to ice cookies for weddings. Here are some of our favorite designs.

We normally ice only in pale ivory and pastel shades, but the colors can be as bright as you like. And the favors can all be made totally personal. We have been asked to make baby footballs, pink elephants, top hats, motorcycles, and ballet shoes. You can add initials or names and dates, too.

Follow all the usual rules for icing and have a look at our packaging section (see pages 141–43) for inspiring ideas for wrapping them up.

Themes

Alphabet & Numbers

Say whatever you want with this simple-to-ice selection of letters and numbers. You can tell it how it is, spell out your messages of love, ice the initials of all your friends, say "Thank you," "I'm sorry," "Get well soon," or "21 to-day." Here are just a few ways to decorate your cookies.

cutters

letters
numbers
(or cut rectangles and ice your letters and numbers onto them)

recipes

1 quantity Super Chocolatey Cookies dough (see page 34) or Vanilla Cookies dough (see page 36); number of cookies will depend on size of cutters, makes approx. 20 x 2–3in letters

1 quantity Basic Royal Icing (see page 21)

line icing

white
red
baby blue
gentian blue
forest green

flooding icing

Aegean blue
red
white
forest green

embellishments

only if you want to

polka dots

Ice around outside of your letter or number in line color of your choice. Allow to dry for at least 5 minutes. * Flood middle with a contrasting color, but don't overfill. * Ice on polka dots immediately with white line icing for a glossy finish.

striped

Ice around outside in line color of your choice. Allow to dry for at least 5 minutes. * Flood with a contrasting color—try not to overfill. * Pipe the stripes immediately with white line icing for a glossy finish.

contrasts

Pipe around outside with line icing color of your choice. Allow to dry for 5 minutes. Flood with a contrasting color.

patchwork

Ice around outline in your chosen color. Allow to dry for 5 minutes. * Flood with same color—try not to overfill. * Pipe on polka dots in white line icing immediately. Leave until set. * Ice "stitches" around outside in a contrasting color of line icing.

flag

Lots of flags have quite tricky patterns, so we use only line icing. * Print an image of your chosen flag and place your cookie in the middle of it. (This will help you to recreate the pattern on the cookie.)

Tips: Letter and number cookies can be a little fragile, so if you need to mail these cookies, perhaps just ice onto squares or rectangles. If you find it tricky to get the flooding icing into all the corners of the letter and number shapes, just push it around with a toothpick to exactly where it needs to be.

Cakes & Cupcakes

Like the treats in the window of the best bakery in town, these glossy little cakes, pastries, and strawberry tarts look so tempting.

cutters

cupcake (see page 153)
tart
circle (for doughnuts)
éclair (see page 153)

recipes

1 quantity orange flavored Plain Cookie dough (see page 33); makes 4 tarts, 4 cupcakes, and 2 each of the other designs

1 quantity Basic Royal Icing (see page 21)

line icing

ivory
donkey brown
red
mustard yellow
baby pink
teddy brown

flooding icing

ivory
red
teddy brown
baby pink
donkey brown

embellishments

anything goes—sprinkles, flowers, baubles, or glitter

cupcakes

Make them up in your favorite colors or ice outline of cupcake case in ivory line icing. * Flood case with ivory. Allow to set. * Add donkey brown line details to case. * Squeeze flooding icing (without an outline) onto the top of the cake just as if you were icing a real cake. Allow to set. * Add iced decorations or other sprinkles.

chocolate and strawberry tarts

Ice outlines of the strawberries in red line and the tart case in donkey brown line. Allow to dry for 5 minutes. * Flood the strawberries with red and the base with teddy brown. Immediately add seed detail to strawberries with yellow line. Leave to set. Pipe lines on tart case in donkey brown.

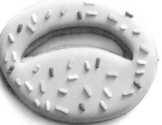

doughnuts

Pipe outline of icing and hole in pink line. Allow to set. * Flood with pink. * When set add sprinkles by piping tiny little lines onto the surface of the icing.

éclairs

Ice around outline of éclair in ivory line. Add the outline of the chocolate with donkey brown line. Allow to dry for 5 minutes. * Flood the chocolate of the éclair with donkey brown flooding icing and the pastry with teddy brown line icing. Rough light brown icing up with knife or spatula to make it look like choux pastry.

Cat & Mouse

These are the Biscuiteer cats. You can ice yours in any shade you like, or add your own kitty's favorite toy.

cutters

cat
circle (for ball of wool)
mouse
goldfish bowl
fish bones (see page 150)
milk bottle (see page 151)

recipes

1 quantity Plain Cookie dough (see page 33) or Super Chocolatey Cookies dough (see page 34); makes about 16

1 quantity Basic Royal Icing (see page 21)

line icing

black
white
baby pink
orange

flooding icing

white
black
orange

tom cat

Outline in black line and leave to dry for 5 minutes. * Put a little blob of white flooding icing on cheek and at tip of tail and ears if you wish. While still wet, fill rest of cat with black flooding icing. With tip of toothpick, "feather" icings so they blend together. Leave to dry. * Add eye with white line icing and black line and nose in pink.

ball of wool

Ice strands of wool in line icing over and over until it looks like a ball of wool.

mouse

Outline in white. Allow to dry for 5 minutes. * Flood mouse in white. Leave to set. * Add tiny spot of black for eye, and nose and tail in baby pink.

goldfish bowl

Ice outline in white and flood with white. Allow to dry. * Pipe a goldfish in orange line, the rim of the bowl in black, and the water line in white. * Flood goldfish with orange. Add dot in black line for the fish's eye.

fish bones

Ice all of the fish bones using white line icing. * Add a black dot for the eye.

milk bottle

Ice around outline in black and allow to dry for 5 minutes. * Flood with white and allow to set. * Use black line to add details to neck of bottle and add "MILK" across center.

Best in Show

We think that these two extremes in the canine club actually look rather lovely together and would both win "best in class" prizes. Our friendly hounds have been chosen to show that you can ice chic puffy poodles to all-butch bull terriers, and anything in between. Add old-fashioned kennels, bouncy balls, and baskets to the collection if you wish.

cutters

terrier
bowl
poodles (see page 146)
bone

recipes

1 quantity Super Chocolatey Cookies dough (see page 34); makes at least 15

1 quantity Basic Royal Icing (see page 21)

line icing

white
black
gentian blue
fuchsia
violet

flooding icing

black
white
gentian blue
baby pink
violet

embellishments

silver and gold baubles
purple glitter sugar

terrier

Pipe around outline in white line icing and leave to dry for 5 minutes. * Add areas of black flooding icing where you want to have markings. Flood rest of body with white. Burst any little air bubbles in white icing with the tip of a toothpick. Gently tap cookie to even out surface. Allow to set. * Pipe on eye, ear, and nose detail in black line. Add a collar set with little silver baubles for studs if you like.

bowl

Pipe outline and rim of bowl in gentian blue line icing. Leave to dry for 5 minutes. * Flood in gentian blue. * When set ice bone in white line.

poodles

All three poodles are basically iced in the same way. Pipe around outline in line icing and allow to dry for 5 minutes. * Flood with appropriate color and leave to set. * Add nose and eye detail using line icing. * For pink poodle add extra fuchsia pink outline for ears and pipe little spots in violet line icing for collar if you like. * For purple pooch pipe on a little violet line icing where you want glitter. While icing is still wet shake on purple glitter and leave to dry. Tap off any excess glitter. * Pipe white line icing on feet, tail, and ears on black poodle. Add collars if you like.

bone

Ice around the outside of the bone in fuchsia, white, or black line. * Leave to dry for 5 minutes then flood with appropriate color icing.

Fashion Bags

We don't think that it is possible to have too many bags.
Here are a few that we rather like, to add to your collection.
They use all sorts of different icing methods that you can
try out if you want to become a handbag designer, too.

cutters

vintage tote
beach basket (see page 147)
clutch bag (see page 151)
smart bag

recipes

1 quantity Super Chocolatey
Cookies dough (see page 34);
if all your bags are large, makes
approx. 12–14, use trimmings to
make purses or key rings

1 quantity Basic Royal Icing
(see page 21)

line icing

violet
bright yellow
donkey brown
red
baby pink
white
lime green

flooding icing

lime green
violet
donkey brown
white

embellishments

gold baubles

vintage tote

Pipe around bag in violet line. Allow to
dry for 5 minutes. * Flood lime green—
use just enough to cover cookie.
Add violet and donkey brown spots
in flooding icing. Allow to set. * Add
further pattern with brightly colored
line icing and add handles using
violet line.

beach basket

Outline the basket shape and opening
at the top in bright yellow line icing.
* Fill front of bag as "knitted" texture
in donkey brown line. Leave to dry
for 5 minutes. * Flood opening with
white. Allow to set. * Pipe lining with
multicolored stripes and add straps,
all in line icing.

clutch bag

Pipe in pink around outline of bag.
* Using pink line icing first, ice on
the swirly pattern to look like knitted
fabric. Fill in the gaps with white line.
* Add clasp and hinge details with
donkey brown line and finish by
adding gold baubles to clasp or
a couple of dots of bright yellow.

very smart bag

Use donkey brown line to pipe all line
details including the strap and leave
to set. * Flood "leather" area with
donkey brown flooding icing and
rest of bag with white flooding icing.
* Then leave to set and add clasp
and bauble details in bright yellow
line icing. * Finally add the edge of
the flap detail in donkey brown line.

smart purple bag

Pipe a violet line around "fabric" part
of bag. Leave to dry for 5 minutes.
* Flood with violet. Leave to set.
* Pipe seam details and handle in
violet line. Add white line icing where
handle joins the bag and for the clasp.
* Add dots in bright yellow line icing
or add golden baubles and a tiny
lime green dot on clasp.

Fashion Shoes

This is your chance to add six new pairs of shoes to your collection in one day. Bake these for your girlfriends, give them to your mother, send them to your sister, but don't expect the men in your life to understand the fascination.

cutters

wedges
knitted boots (see page 149)
party shoes
spike heels
sneakers

recipes

1 quantity Molasses Spice Cookies dough (see page 39); makes approx. 14 cookies depending on which pairs you make

1 quantity Basic Royal Icing (see page 21)

line icing

grape
rose
black
baby pink
white
lime green

flooding icing

lime green
white
red

embellishments

colored glitter sugar

wedges

Ice sole with grape line icing. * Use rose line icing to outline "leather" area, including peep toe, strap, and inside of shoe. Leave to dry for 5 minutes. * Flood "leather" area with lime green. Allow to set. * Add buckles or flowers to front in your favorite bright line icing.

knitted boots

Ice on classic crêpe sole using black line icing. * Create "knitted" texture in light rose line icing all the way up boots. Change angle of "knitting" so it looks like the real thing. Allow this to dry briefly. * Use baby pink line to add heel details and black line to add the buttons.

party shoes

Pipe around outline and also top edge of shoe in bright line icing. Leave to dry for 5 minutes. * Flood soon-to-be sequined area with white. Allow to dry for 1 minute. * Sprinkle with glitter sugar. Tap off excess once set. * Add bow or buckle of top seam detail in line icing.

spike heels

Pipe heel, sole, and straps in grape line icing. Leave to set. * Fill in between lines of straps in white line icing. Add lime line to sole area and heel and allow to dry. * To add sparkle detail, pipe tiny spots of white line icing down front of shoe and sprinkle with glitter while still wet. Tap off excess when icing is dry.

sneakers

Ice outline of red area in rose line icing. Use white line icing to add sole and tip of shoe. Leave to dry for 5 minutes. * Flood shoe with red. Allow to set. * Pipe on eyelets, sole detail, and ventilation holes with fine black line. * Use white line to add logo background, seam details, and laces. * Pipe on your initial or logo in grape.

Presents for the Teacher

These cookies make a lovely present for anything to do with school. Say thank you to your child's teacher or send exam good luck wishes or congratulations for getting into college. If completing the whole collection looks a little complicated, just a selection of bright and beautiful pencils looks lovely. Choose a pretty mug to pack them in for a luxury tea and cookies gift!

cutters

paper
school bus
apple (see page 153)
ruler
protractor
palette
pencil (see page 149)
blackboard

recipes

1 quantity of the recipient's favorite cookie dough; makes at least 16

1 quantity Basic Royal Icing (see page 21)

line icing

white
red
gentian blue
bright yellow
black
donkey brown
forest green
orange

flooding icing

white
bright yellow
red
forest green
orange
baby blue
black

paper

Ice around outline and holes in paper in white line and allow to dry for 5 minutes. * Flood whole page with white. Pop any little bubbles that appear with tip of a toothpick and tap cookie to even out the surface. * Before icing has chance to set, add fine red line for margin and fine blue icing for lines on paper.

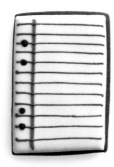

school bus

Ice around outline, windows, sign, headlights, and mirror details in yellow line icing. Leave to dry for 5 minutes. * Flood body with yellow and the sign and headlights with white. Allow to set. * Add "School Bus" lettering, bumpers, wipers, and wheels in black line icing.

apple

Pipe around outline of apple in red, remembering to include bite mark. Add stalk in brown and leaf outline in green. Leave to dry for 5 minutes. * Flood apple with red and the leaf with forest green.

ruler, protractor, & palette

These three are all iced in the same way. Pipe white line icing all around the outside and let it dry for 5 minutes. * Flood whole shape with white icing and pop any air bubbles. Leave to set. * Use black line icing to add details.

pencil

Pipe black outline around pencil. Add a line where it has been sharpened to and pipe "lead" of pencil in a bright color. Leave to dry for 5 minutes. * Flood pencil with chosen color and the wooden area with white. Leave to set. * Pipe detail on the pencil in black line.

blackboard

Use brown line icing to pipe border around edge of blackboard. Leave to dry for 5 minutes. * Flood rectangle with black icing. Leave to set. * Use white line and flooding icing to "draw" on blackboard.

On Safari

We have rounded up all of our favorite animals for this safari collection, but you might like to add some more of your own.

cutters

lion
parrot
rhino
giraffe
crocodile
butterfly (see page 151)
tiger
mommy & baby elephant

recipes

1 quantity Super Chocolatey Cookies dough (see page 34); makes 14–16

1 quantity Basic Royal Icing (see page 21)

line icing

orange
bright yellow
donkey brown
red
gray
black
white
forest green
fucshia

flooding icing

bright yellow
orange
baby blue
white
red
gray
forest green
fucshia

lion

Ice the mane in orange line icing using lots of little swirly movements. * Use yellow line to outline face and body. Allow to dry for 5 minutes. * Flood with yellow. Leave to set. * Add paws and leg details in yellow, an orange tip to the tail, and a nose in donkey brown line.

parrot

Outline parrot in red line icing. Add lines between different color areas in red line. Leave to set for 5 minutes. * Fill individual areas with flooding icing and allow to dry briefly. * Add feet, eye, and beak details, and red line overpiping to wing and head.

rhino

Outline rhino body in gray. * Allow to set then flood with gray flooding icing. * When dry add horn, toe, eye, and ear details in black and white line icing.

giraffe

Outline all around shape in bright yellow line icing. Leave to dry for 5 minutes. * Flood with yellow but don't overfill. Before yellow icing sets, add markings in donkey brown line and allow to dry. * Add eye and tail in black and white line.

crocodile

Ice around outside of crocodile in forest green. Allow to dry for 5 minutes. * Flood with forest green. Leave to set. * Pipe teeth with white line, feet detail in brown line, eyes in black and white line, and the pattern on skin in forest green line.

butterfly

These can be any color you like. Pipe the body and wing outline in line icing. Allow to dry for 5 minutes. * Flood wings with same color icing. Allow to set. * Add spots and patterns in lots of bright colors using flooding and line icing.

tiger

Outline tiger shape in black and allow to dry. * Add white flooding icing on belly, ears, and muzzle then flood rest of body in orange flooding icing and leave to set. * Use line icing to pipe lots of black stripes and markings all over. * Add face details in black line.

mommy & baby elephant

Pipe gray line around elephant shape. Allow to dry for 5 minutes. * Flood with gray. Leave to dry briefly, then add tusks, eye, and feet in white line. * Add ear detail in gray line and a black dot on the eye.

Biscuiteers Circus

These bright and beautiful cookies recreate the scene of an old-fashioned circus. We love their gaudy colors and are very proud of our clever seal and dancing elephant. Vary the palette if you like, but our Biscuiteers' circus always performs well in these vibrant colors.

cutters

sad clown
sea lion
elephant
carriage
ringmaster's coat
big top/sideshow booth

recipes

1 quantity orange flavored Super Chocolatey Biscuits dough (see page 34); makes approx. 12 cookies

1 quantity Basic Royal Icing (see page 21)

line icing

black
red
gray
white
bright yellow

flooding icing

white
raspberry
gray
red
orange
bright yellow

sad clown

Ice around outline in black line icing. Allow to dry for 5 minutes. * Flood whole clown in white. Burst any little bubbles in white icing with the tip of a toothpick. Leave to set. * Use black line to add all details and pattern to the clown's outfit. * Use red line icing to add mouth and tears.

sea lion

Ice around ball in red line icing and add segments in middle. * Use red line icing to pipe around stand in zigzag pattern. * Ice outline of sea lion in gray. Leave to dry for 5 minutes. * Add raspberry and white flooding icing to ball, flood sea lion with gray, and stand with white and red. Allow to set. * Use line icing to add white dot on ball, white top and red dots on stand, and a twinkly eye and wet nose in black.

elephant

Ice around elephant in gray line icing. Allow to dry for 5 minutes. * Flood elephant with gray and leave to set. * Use red line to outline ball and stripes across it, headdress, and blanket. Allow to set briefly then squeeze raspberry flooding icing into headdress, blanket, and stripe on ball. * Add yellow detail in line icing to feathers on headdress. * Flood ball with red.

carriage

Ice around outline, including wheels, in yellow line icing. Leave to set for 5 minutes. * Fill with red flooding icing and allow to dry briefly. * Add animal to the carriage (we used white line with black detail for our polar bear). * Use yellow line to add bars, decorations, and details.

ringmaster's coat

Ice all black details, apart from bow tie and buttons, using black line icing. Allow to dry for 5 minutes. * Carefully use flooding icing to fill in red for coat, orange for vest, bright yellow for collar, and white for shirt. Leave to set. * Add the buttons and bow tie in black line icing.

big top/sideshow booths

Pipe on lines and fill in with red and white line icing. Allow to set. * Add carpet with red line and interior in black. * Add flag and banner details in line, too.

Toys for Big Boys

We don't want to stereotype the boys in our lives…
but we thought that this sports collection and the
ice cold beer are enough to keep them amused for hours.

cutters

football cleats
beer glass
circles for soccer,
cricket, and tennis balls
tennis racket
cricket bat (see page 151)

recipes

Great made from crunchy
Peanut Butter Cookies dough
(see page 39); makes approx.
15 cookies

1 quantity Basic Royal Icing
(see page 21)

line icing

red
white
forest green
teddy brown
black
bright yellow

flooding icing

red
mustard yellow
white
black
bright yellow
ivory

football cleats

Outline the shape of the cleat in red line,
remembering to add the line around
the opening of the cleat. Leave to dry.
* Flood with red runny icing and allow
to set. * Add all the details of laces,
moldings, cleats, and logo using red,
white, and forest green line icing.

beer glass

Use white line to outline all around
the outside, and between the beer
and the head. Let this dry for
5 minutes. * Flood the glass with
mustard yellow runny icing and the
top with white runny icing. * When
this is dry, use another layer of white
flooding icing to add the head and
gloss to the glass and add teddy brown
lines to define the base of the glass.

soccer ball

Make the hexagonal pattern on the ball
using white line icing and leave to dry.
* Flood the sections in black and white
to create the classic soccer ball pattern.

tennis racket

Use red and white line icing to
outline the racket and black for
the handle area. Use black line
to add the strings. * When this
is dry, flood the frame and handle
with red, white, and black.

Tennis ball: outline the ball in
bright yellow line and leave to dry.
* Flood with runny yellow icing
and add the white details when
it has dried.

cricket bat

Use white line icing to outline the bat,
and red to fill the whole handle and
leave to dry. * Flood the bat with ivory
runny icing and add detail using
black line.

Cricket ball: outline in red and leave
to dry. * Flood with red runny icing and
add details in white line when it is dry.

In the Garden

Everything is always perfect in the Biscuiteers' garden, just as long as we keep the creepy crawlies away from our lovely flowers and the vegetable patch.

cutters

watering can
spade
trowel
fork
boots
flowerpot
carrot
leek
tomato

recipes

1 quantity orange flavored Plain Cookies dough (see page 33); makes at least 25

1 quantity Basic Royal Icing (see page 21)

line icing

gentian blue
teddy brown
forest green
red
white
black (tiny amount)
primrose

flooding icing

baby blue
teddy brown
forest green
orange
white
red

watering can

Ice outline of can, spout, and handle in gentian blue line icing and allow to set for 5 minutes. * Flood can with baby blue and leave to dry. * Overpipe all lines and details on can in gentian blue line icing.

spade/trowel/fork

These are all iced in same way. Pipe all outlines of handles using brown line and shapes of tools using gentian blue line. Leave to dry for 5 minutes. * Fill the handles with brown flooding icing and the tools with baby blue. Let these set before adding any surface details with gentian blue line.

boots

Pipe outline and heel in green line and leave to dry for 5 minutes. * Flood with green and allow to set. * Ice on ridges, seams, and tie in green, label in red, and white and buckle in black line.

flowerpot

Pipe outline in brown, including shape of rim. Use primrose, forest green, and white line icing to add flowers and leaves. Leave to dry for 5 minutes. * Flood pot with runny teddy brown icing. * Add details in brown line.

carrot

Using line icing, pipe leaves at top in green and add a red outline around the outside. Leave to dry for 5 minutes. * Flood whole of carrot in orange and leave to set. * Add details in red line.

leek

Outline bottom of leek in white and leaves in green line icing. Allow to set. * Flood leaves with green and bottom of leek with white. Leave to set. * Pipe little roots in brown line and leaf details in green.

tomato

Ice outline in red. Leave to dry for 5 minutes. * Flood with red and leave to set. * Pipe on stalk in green.

Flower Power

These are fantastic cookies for beginners. They can be as simple or as complicated as you like and you can use pretty much any colors you please. You can use flower-shaped cookie cutters, plain and fluted round cutters, or improvise by carefully pressing different-sized glasses into your dough and cutting circles.

cutters

flowers (see page 148) or plain/ fluted circles
leaf (see tip)

recipes

1 quantity Super Chocolatey Cookies dough (see page 34); makes 20–24 cookies

1 quantity Basic Royal Icing (see page 21)

line icing

white
raspberry
deep-sea blue
forest green
orange
violet
bright yellow

flooding icing

raspberry
parma violet
pink
bright yellow
orange

embellishments

gold and silver baubles
silver glitter sugar

starburst flower

Use white line to ice a fat circle in the middle and fill center with raspberry line. * Add petals in deep-sea blue line.

pink passion flower

Ice two circles in raspberry in center of flower like a bullseye. * Flood center with raspberry and outer ring with parma violet. * Ice petal shapes around outside in raspberry line. * Fill petals with pink flooding icing. Allow to dry for at least 2 minutes. * Use white line icing to make stamen pattern and then line ice around this in raspberry.

daisy

Ice a line of touching dots around center of the flower. Add spiky petals in raspberry line and allow to dry. * Flood center in bright yellow flooding icing and add final spot details in green line.

Tip: We sometimes bake our cookies spiked onto wooden skewers. If you want to try this, use a lower temperature oven 275°F for 25 minutes so the sticks don't burn.

retro orange flower

Ice a white circle of dots in middle of cookie and a stylized petal pattern around the outside of the flower. * Fill middle with yellow flooding icing and petals with orange runny icing. * Allow to dry. * Pipe on green center, orange dots, and green line pattern.

shamrock

Ice around outside in violet line. * Fill with parma violet flooding icing. Allow to dry. * Use yellow line to ice a ring of touching dots and fill inside with raspberry flooding icing. Allow to dry. * Decorate raspberry area with a circle of white line icing.

Tip: We make lovely little leaves to go with our flowers. You can buy leaf cutters or simply use an overlapping circle cutter to make the same shape. If you are making these cookies for eagle-eyed children, try adding the odd bite to the leaves and a few little caterpillars to see if anyone notices.

Vintage Summer

These lovely cookies sum up summer in Blighty.
There is a little festival chic alongside summer fair fun.
If the Union Jack bunting is a little too tricky for you,
just make some with polka dots instead.

cutters

triangle (for bunting)
boots
strawberry (see page 147)
oval (for mug)
camper van

recipes

1 quantity Hazelnut Cookies
dough (see page 37);
makes at least 20, use
trimmings to make lots
of luscious strawberries

1 quantity Basic Royal Icing
(see page 21)

line icing

white
gentian blue
red
bright yellow
forest green
raspberry
black

flooding icing

red
gentian blue
white
raspberry

bunting

Ice all white lines on the biscuit first
then add the corresponding line icing
around outside of the bunting. Leave to
dry. * Flood cross in red and remainder
in blue. Allow to set. * Use line icing in
blue and red to complete flag.

boots

Add any pattern you like to your
boots—we have used dots. Use yellow
line to outline patterned area of boot.
Leave to dry for 5 minutes. * Flood with
white and leave to dry. Add little dots
of red line icing, buckles, and tags if
you desire.

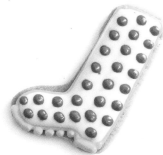

Tip: If you would like to hang your
bunting cut a hole using a large
drinking straw before you bake.
Ice around the hole and follow the
rest of instructions. When dry thread
through pretty ribbon and hang!

strawberry

Pipe stem and leaves in green line
icing and outline berry in red. Allow to
dry for 5 minutes. * Flood the berry
with red and immediately pipe on tiny
seeds with yellow line icing.

mug

Use white line to ice round mug,
stripes and rim. Allow to set for
5 minutes. * Flood alternate stripes
with blue and white.

camper van

Ice around the white shape in white
line icing, including squares for
windows, bumper, and headlights.
* Add raspberry outline and allow to
dry for 5 minutes. * Use raspberry and
white flooding icing to fill the two areas.
Leave to set. * Pipe the wheels, hubcaps,
headlights, and symbols in line icing.
Add frames to windows in black.

Seaside Summer

We do like to be beside the seaside at Biscuiteers. So we made this very vintage collection with all the beaches that we have ever been to in mind. Add your own umbrellas, frisbees, beach balls, and picnics or whatever it is that sums up a day at the beach for you.

cutters

kite
bikini
seagull
beach cabana (see page 146)
ice cream (see page 146)
starfish
bucket & spade (see page 146)

recipes

1 quantity Simple Butter Cookies dough (see page 37) or Super Chocolatey dough (see page 34); makes 14-18 cookies
1 quantity Basic Royal Icing (see page 21)

line icing

bright yellow
gentian blue
red
black
white
orange
pea green
donkey brown

flooding icing

bright yellow
gentian blue
red
white
orange

embellishments

use brown glitter sugar for the sand and candy shoe laces for the ice cream

kite

Ice the quarters of the kite and the string for the tail in yellow line icing. * Allow to set then flood quarters in yellow and gentian blue. * Leave these to set then add the tail's colored bows in line icing.

polka dot bikini

Use red line to ice outline of the bikini. * Leave to set then flood with runny red icing until just full. * Add spots of white runny icing before the red has set.

seagull

Use line icing all over in black and white to make the seagull's body and feathers. * Allow to dry then finish with an orange beak and a little black dot for the eye.

beach cabana

This is iced in line icing only. Start with the white outline of the shape of the beach cabana and door. * Then fill in all the stripes first in pea green and then in white. * Allow to set fully then use white line icing to ice on the area of sand at the front. * Sprinkle immediately with brown glitter sugar and allow to dry. * Add a little plaque for your beach cabana name and a black line door handle. * When these have set, ice on your name in black line.

ice cream

Use donkey brown line to ice the pattern of the cones. * Leave to set then use colored line icing thickly applied for the scoops of ice cream in your favorite flavor and a chocolate candy in donkey brown line. * Sprinkle on the candy shoe laces before the icing has set.

starfish

Outline and flood in orange, pea green, or yellow. * Allow to dry then add spot and eye details in black and white line icing.

bucket

Outline in yellow line adding rim and corner details to the bucket. Leave to dry. * Flood all over with yellow runny icing. Leave to set. * Add a bit more runny icing where you want the sand and dust with brown glitter sugar. * When dry add the bucket handle detail in white line.

spade

Outline in yellow line and leave to dry. * Flood with runny yellow icing and sprinkle the brown glitter sugar on the spade tip for sand. * Leave to dry.

London

This is home ground for Biscuiteers. We have cherrypicked our favorite London icons and iced them just for you. Add a few of your own landmarks, too. Buildings are particularly good as you can just ice them onto easy-to-cut squares and rectangles.

cutters

circle (for Tube sign)
taxi
telephone booth
mailbox
Big Ben
London Bridge
oval (for London Eye)

recipes

1 quantity Super Chocolatey Cookies dough (see page 34); makes at least 15 cookies

1 quantity Basic Royal Icing (see page 21)

line icing

bright yellow
white
black
gray
red
teddy brown
donkey brown
gentian blue

flooding icing

gentian blue
white
red
black
teddy brown

Tube sign

Ice yellow line around rectangular nameplate and outer circle. Ice around inner circle in white. Allow to dry for 5 minutes. * Flood nameplate in blue, inner circle in white, and outer circle in red. Leave to set.   Pipe name in black.

taxi

Pipe outline of bodywork and windows in black line, leaving space to ice on wheels later. Leave to dry for 5 minutes. * Flood with black. * Add wheels in black line icing. Leave to set. * Fill windows and add a radiator cover with gray line icing. Use line icing to add all other details.

telephone booth

Pipe all red line details and pipe base outline in black. Allow to dry for 5 minutes. * Flood top of box with red and base with black. Flood light at top with white. (Leave windows uniced.)

mailbox

Ice top of box in red line and base in black line and lines in between. * When dry flood top with red and base with black. Allow to dry. * Use red, black, and white line icings to add details.

Big Ben

Outline whole shape in white line and leave to set. * Flood with white runny icing and, when dry, use teddy and donkey brown and gray line icing to add bricks and clock face.

London Bridge

Look carefully at a picture of the bridge before you ice it. Use donkey brown line to add all outlines for stone sections, including line down center of each pillar that divides teddy brown and white flooding icing. Leave a gap for walkway. Leave to dry for about 5 minutes. Flood base of pillars and left-hand side in teddy brown and right in white. Allow to dry. * Use brown line to add detail to pillars. * Add all blue and white line details that make up remainder of bridge.

London Eye

Use white line icing to pipe frame and wheel. * Add spokes and inner frame in gray line. * Ice tiny capsules in black and gray line icing.

Paris

This is our take on the capital of sophistication: Paris. We've included a dainty Parisian poodle and all her favorite landmarks.

cutters

Eiffel Tower
poodle (see page 146)
name plaque
boulangerie
Arc de Triomphe
Notre Dame

recipes

1 quantity Super Chocolatey Cookies dough (see page 34); makes at least 15, add poodles from trimmings

1 quantity Basic Royal Icing (see page 21)

line icing

Aegean blue
leaf green
black
baby pink
gray
white
red

flooding icing

Aegean blue
white
light baby pink
gray

Eiffel Tower

Ice blue outline around triangle. Add rows of grass at base with green line icing. Allow to set for 5 minutes. * Flood background in Aegean blue. Before this sets, add little clouds in white flooding icing. Let this dry for 2 minutes. * Ice structure in black line.

poodle

Pipe around outline in baby pink line and allow to dry for 5 minutes. * Flood entire dog with light baby pink icing and leave to set. * Add nose and bow details in black and pink line.

name plaque

Ice around shape in gray. Add outline of name and district plaques in blue line. Leave to set. * Flood around plaque with gray. Fill in plaque with Aegean blue. Allow to set. * Add text in gray and white, detail lines in white, and the little gray line embellishments.

boulangerie

Use Aegean blue line to ice around top area of store, door, and windows. Use red line to ice along bottom of storefront. Leave to dry for 5 minutes. * Flood sides and sign with white. Leave to set. * Add flowers, door handle, door detail, and "BOULANGERIE" using appropriate colored line. * Our boulangerie is a mini work of art; make yours a little simpler if you wish.

Arc de Triomphe/ Notre Dame

For the Arc de Triomphe ice outline of arc in gray line and edge of cookie in blue line. Allow to dry for 5 minutes. * Flood appropriate areas with white and Aegean blue flooding icing. Leave to set. * Use gray line to add stone details to arch. * Decorate Notre Dame cookie in same way, but without sky background.

New York

There are quite a few colors to mix for this collection, but the icing is relatively straightforward. We have chosen our best bits from the city that never sleeps. You can add your own street names, bridges, bagels, or whatever else that will make it your take on New York.

cutters

taxi
big apple
hot dog
street signs
skyscraper
Statue of Liberty

recipes

1 quantity Super Chocolatey Cookies dough (see pae 34); makes at least 15 cookies, make extra hot dogs or "I heart New York" stickers with any trimmings

1 quantity Basic Royal Icing (see page 21)

line icing

bright yellow
black
gray
white
red
donkey brown
eucalyptus

flooding icing

mustard yellow
red
donkey brown
ivory
forest green
gray
eucalyptus

taxi

Pipe outline of taxi and its windows using yellow line. Don't forget to leave space for wheels. Leave to dry for 5 minutes. * Flood taxi with yellow. Allow to dry briefly. * Pipe black line inside windows, on bumper, and tires. * Add the details in line icing: chrome trim on hubcaps, bumper and windows in gray; white line on license plate and bumper; brake lights in red; "NYC," "AXI," and round circle for "T" in black; "T" in yellow.

big apple

Ice outline of apple in red. Allow to dry for 5 minutes. * Flood with red. Leave to dry. * Pipe in "T" and "NY" in black line, and add white heart and stalk in black line icing.

hot dog

Ice outline of wiener in donkey brown and the bun in white. Allow to dry for 5 minutes. * Flood wiener with donkey brown and the bun with ivory. Leave to set. * Add ketchup and mustard wiggles in red and yellow line icing.

street signs

Outline sign in white and allow to dry for 5 minutes. * Flood with green and leave to dry. * Pipe on street name in white line.

skyscraper

Outline in gray and allow to dry. * Flood with gray and leave to dry. * Pipe all windows, doors, and details using gray line icing.

Statue of Liberty

Ice all of outline, except the flame, using eucalyptus line. Allow to dry. * Flood with eucalyptus. Leave to set. * Add all details in eucalyptus green line. * Ice flame in yellow line and add details to crown in gray line.

Cookie Classics

Here we have a seriously delicious Biscuiteers version of cookie classics. We find that they are too precious and tasty to even consider dunking in our tea.

buttercream recipe

7 tablespoons butter

7oz / 1½ cups confectioners' sugar

Beat these together with your chosen flavoring ingredients until light and fluffy and completely combined. Keep the buttercream covered closely with plastic wrap until you are ready to use it so that it doesn't begin to get hard before you use it.

flavoring buttercream

Vanilla

add a couple of drops of vanilla extract

Chocolate

1–2 tablespoons of sifted cocoa powder

Lemon or orange

add the finely grated zest of 2 oranges or lemons

Coffee

add 1 teaspoon of instant coffee

Vanilla Sandwich Cookies

1 quantity Vanilla Cookies dough (see page 36)

1 quantity vanilla buttercream

1 quantity Basic Royal Icing (see page 21) made into ivory-colored icing (see page 23)

1 piping bag

Cut by hand, or use a rectangular cutter to make 24 Vanilla Cookies. * Cook and cool as per instructions. * Use the line icing to pipe on the details and name to the 12 tops of the cookie in a traditional pattern. * Use an offset spatula to spread buttercream onto the 12 base cookies. * Press the iced cookie tops down onto the buttercream until they are stuck together.

Iced gems

Make these from leftover scraps of dough or icing. Cut and bake a tiny circle and top with icing squeezed through a star nozzle (see page 31 for picture).

Jam Sandwich Cookies

1 quantity Simple Butter Cookies dough (see page 37)

1 quantity of vanilla buttercream

5 tablespoons of your favorite jam

1 round crinkly edged cutter

mini cutters for the center

Cut 24 circles with the larger cutter. * Take half and use the smaller cutters to cut out a little hole in the center * Bake as usual. * When the cookies are totally cool, take the 12 base cookies and pipe a thick ring of icing around all the outside edges of the cookie to make a wall to hold in the jam. * Then spoon a little of your favorite jam into the center of the cookie and spread evenly inside the icing ring. * Squash the top down onto the base until firmly stuck together.

Chocolate Sandwich Cookies

1 quantity Super Chocolatey Cookies dough (see page 34)

1 quantity chocolate buttercream

1 piping bag of donkey brown icing

Hand cut or use a rectangular cutter to make 24 Super Chocolatey Cookies. * Use the prongs on a fork to spike little lines of dots all down the cookies. * Cook and cool as per instructions. * Then pipe the name onto the cookies with the line icing. * Sandwich the cookies together with a big squidge of chocolate buttercream.

Make Oreo Cookies using a similar method, but cut rounds, fill with vanilla buttercream, and pipe on the distinctive Oreo pattern in the donkey brown icing.

Iced ring cookies

1 quantity Vanilla Cookies dough (see page 36)

1 quantity Basic Royal Icing (see page 21), made into 3 colors of flooding icing and pink line icing

1 piping bag

1 large and 1 small round cutter

Use the two cutters to make the ring cookies. Bake and cool as per instructions. * Pipe on the outline in line icing around the edge and center. * Squeeze on the runny flooding icing inside the lines and add spots and lines of different colors. * Feather the icing using the tip of a toothpick.

Creepy Crawlies

We love these creatures. You can make them as friendly or as fierce as you like. We used to make a spider, but it was a little too close to the real thing to be truly enjoyable to eat. These cookies are great for party bags and work well when personalized with initials or names. Stick to the cuter crawlies for younger cookie eaters.

cutters

ladybug
caterpillar
snail
leaf (see page 153)
dragonfly (see page 150)
lizard
frog (see page 150)

recipes

1 quantity Molasses Spice Cookies dough (see page 36); makes 2 of each creature

1 quantity Basic Royal Icing (see page 21)

line icing

black
red
leaf green
baby pink
lime green
eucalyptus
bright yellow
white

flooding icing

red
black
lime green
baby pink
leaf green
baby blue
bright yellow

embellishments

purple sparkly glitter sugar

ladybug

Ice head using black line icing. * Ice outline of shell in red line icing and allow to dry for at least 5 minutes. * Fill shell with red flooding icing (don't overfill). Immediately add spots of black flooding icing. Leave to set. * Add legs, antennae, and line down back of shell in black line icing.

caterpillar

Outline shape with leaf green line icing. Allow to dry for 5 minutes. * Flood middle with lime green and leave to set. * Add segments to body using leaf green line. * Ice on legs, eyes, and antennae in black line.

snail

Ice around outline of body in baby pink. Leave to dry for 5 minutes. * Fill with baby pink flooding icing. * Shell design is made with flooding icing straight onto cookie without any line "walls." Start in middle and swirl icing around. Leave to set. * Add antennae and eyes in black line.

leaf

Ice around outside of leaf and stalk in lime green line icing. Don't forget to add a few little munch marks around edge. Allow the line to dry. * Fill leaf with leaf green flooding icing. Leave to set. * Ice on vein details in lime green line.

dragonfly

Ice body, head, and outline of wings in eucalyptus. Leave to dry for about 5 minutes. * Fill wings with baby blue flooding icing. Allow to set for a minute then sprinkle on purple sparkly glitter sugar. Leave to dry. * Add legs in black line icing.

lizard

Ice all over using leaf green line icing, leaving two small areas for eyes. Allow to dry briefly. Add stripes in bright yellow line. * Pipe eyes in black and white line icing.

frog

Ice outline of frog in leaf green line icing and allow to set. * Flood body and legs with leaf green runny icing until just full then add tiny bright yellow spots in more flooding icing. Leave to dry. * Ice on eyes in black and white line icing.

Cowboys & Indians

These old-fashioned cowboys and Indians cookies appeal to boys of all ages. Cacti have never tasted so good. If you have enough dough, make a whole village of tepees and ice them all differently.

cutters

tepee
boots
horse
cactus
headdress
Stetson

recipes

1 quantity orange flavored Super Chocolatey Cookies (see page 34) dough; makes 2 pairs of boots, 4 cacti, 1 horse, 1 headdress, 1 Stetson, 1 tepee, 5 arrows, 1 revolver

1 quantity Basic Royal Icing (see page 21)

line icing

donkey brown
black
red
bright yellow
gentian blue
white
ivory (make it dark)
forest green
lime green

flooding icing

ivory (make it dark)
forest green
sage green

tepee

Ice outline in donkey brown line and allow to dry for 5 minutes. * Flood with ivory and let dry until surface is hard. * Add wooden poles at top in black line. * Ice patterns in red, yellow, and blue line.

boots

Ice around outline of boot in donkey brown. Allow to dry for 5 minutes. * Flood with ivory. Allow to set. * Ice the seams with brown line icing. Add the heel with lines of brown and the stitching detail in white.

horse

Ice around outside with dark ivory line. Allow to dry for 5 minutes. * Flood with ivory and allow to set. * Using line icing add saddle in multicolors and tail in brown. * Ice on hooves and eye and ear details in brown line.

cactus

Outline in forest green line and leave to dry for 5 minutes. * Fill with forest green flooding icing and allow to dry. * Add lines or spines in lime green line icing.

headdress

Made using only line icing. Use white to pipe on headband and white parts of feathers. * Add red and forest green tips to feathers and use yellow for feather quills.

Stetson

Ice around outline in donkey brown. Allow to dry for 5 minutes. * Flood with sage green and allow to set.

Pirate Party

These work beautifully as favors for pirate parties.
Ice your own little pirates in their favorite T-shirts
among this bloodthirsty crew.

cutters

pirate
pirate ship
treasure chest
circle (for skull and crossbones)
palm tree
cutlass

recipes

1 quantity of your little
pirate's favorite dough;
makes 14–18 cookies

1 quantity Basic Royal Icing
(see page 21)

line icing

black
white
red
orange
Aegean blue
donkey brown
mustard yellow
leaf green

flooding icing

black
white
red
donkey brown
leaf green

embellishments

gold and silver glitter sugar

pirate

Ice one area at a time. Use black outline
to pipe around hat, hook, hand, stump,
and foot. Leave to dry for 2 minutes.
* Flood hat with black. * Pipe white
outline of shirt and red outline of shorts,
leaving a gap for a belt in between.
Allow to dry. * Flood shirt in white and
shorts in red. Leave to set. * Pipe on
big bushy orange beard in line icing.
Add face and ears in white line. * Ice
on details of belt, grin, eyepatch, eye,
hat, and stripes on the shirt. Ice the first
mate in different combinations!

pirate ship

Outline hull and forecastle in brown line,
remembering to add castlelike details.
* Outline sail in white line and add
stripes across it. Allow to dry. * Flood
hull and castle with brown. Add red and
white stripes to sail with flooding icing.
Leave to set. * Pipe on castle bricks,
stripes, and portholes on the hull. Add a
Jolly Roger in black and white line icing
and an anchor in yellow and black.

treasure chest

Use brown line icing to pipe all outlines
of the trunk. Make sure that it looks
open and has space for some booty!
Allow to set. * Flood the outside of
the trunk with brown. Let this set
completely. * Pipe the treasure area
with yellow and let it set for a minute
before adding golden glitter. * Add
bands, lock, and handles in yellow
line icing.

skull and crossbones

Outline detail of the skull in black line.
Remember to add face details. Leave
to set. Flood skull and bones with white
icing. * Pop any little bubbles below
the surface with a toothpick.

palm tree

Ice outline of trunk in brown
and outlines of leaves in leaf
green. Leave to dry for 5 minutes.
* Flood trunk in brown and leaves
in green. Allow to set. * Add details
of trunk, leaves, and coconuts in
brown and green line.

cutlass

Outline blade in white line icing
and pipe grip in yellow. Allow to
dry. * Flood cutlass blade with
white. Let dry for 1 minute and
then sprinkle on silver glitter.

Toy Box

These toys are all our favorites and we're sure you won't mind tidying them up. You don't have to make them all—you can mix and match.

cutters

race car (see page 152)
xylophone
plane (see page 152)
train (see page 152)
Russian dolls (see page 152)

recipes

1 quantity Simple Butter Cookies dough (see page 37); makes approx. 17 cookies

1 quantity Basic Royal Icing (see page 21)

line icing

red
donkey brown
orange
leaf green
Aegean blue
bright yellow
baby pink
white

flooding icing

bright yellow
orange
leaf green
Aegean blue
red
white

embellishments

silver baubles

race car

Ice outline and filling of tires in red. * Choose your own car color then ice around body in line icing and leave to dry. * Fill with colored flooding icing and allow to set. * Add a little circle of yellow flooding icing to side of car. When set add number detail and steering wheel.

xylophone

Ice outline of bars with different colored line icing. Allow to dry for 5 minutes. * Fill with corresponding flooding icing. * Add detail and beaters in brown line icing. Use a little silver bauble for end of beater if you wish.

plane

Outline each section of the plane in different colored line icing. Allow to dry then flood each area with the same color flooding icing. Add plane details with line icing.

train

Ice all outlines and borders of colored areas in red line icing. Allow to dry for 5 minutes. * Fill in blocks of color using flooding icing and leave to set briefly. * Add details of windows and lines down the engine's tank.

Russian dolls

Using five different colors, pipe on oval face on each doll in line icing. Add outline of dolls' bodies and allow to set. * Squeeze on flooding icing for each color of doll and leave to dry. * Add details of eyes, cheeks, buttons, lips, noses, and curls and any pattern to the dolls' bodies.

Little Girl's Fairy Party

Don't expect anyone over the age of ten to actually want to eat more than a couple of the totally glittery cookies. The first pair of glitter shoes that we iced are framed and still look fabulous after about five years.

cutters

ring
party shoes
wand
wings
tiara
butterfly (see page 151)
tutu

recipes

1 quantity Vanilla Cookies dough (see page 36) (good if cookies need to travel), or try Simple Butter Cookies dough (see page 37) (not as sweet); makes about 15 cookies, make lots of rings with trimmings

1 quantity Basic Royal Icing (see page 21)

line icing

baby pink
white
parma violet

flooding icing

baby pink
white
parma violet

embellishments

silver, pink, purple, and other colored glitter
pink sugar crystals
colored baubles
(basically anything goes!)

party shoes

Ice the outline of the shoe, heel, and strap in baby pink line icing. * Leave to dry then flood center of shoe in pink and sprinkle with colored glitter.

butterfly

Pipe the wings in fine lacy white line pattern. Sprinkle with silver glitter. * When dry add pink details to outside of wings and body.

wand & wings

Ice wand and wing shape in white and baby pink icing, including any patterns, in white line icing. Immediately add silver sprinkle glitter. Tap off any excess when dry. * Add baubles using a little white line icing as glue.

tiara

Use same method for tiara as for the wand and wings. However, ice all pink glitter areas first and add pink glitter. * Allow this to dry totally before icing more pattern with parma violet and decorating this with purple glitter.

tutu

Start by icing the tutu outline in parma violet line. Leave to set then flood with parma violet runny icing. Add little sugar crystals and leave to set. * Pipe on frill at hem in line icing and add pink dot and belt background. Finally add pink dot details to belt and cover in pink sugar crystals.

Tip: Glitter sticks only to wet icing. Make sure that all the background areas are totally dry before you add icing to the areas where you want to stick your glitter.

Bake with Mother

Most children can ice some simple lines onto the cookies, and no children we know can resist trying lots of the icing. Choose how much they want to be involved with the preparation depending on their age. For tiny tots squeezing a few final lines of icing is probably where to start, but older children can normally manage to take on the whole cookie. For when time is short, buy and store in the pantry ready-to-use tubes of icing, available in white and several colors for impromptu icing on rainy days. There are several other collections in the book that are good for minis to ice, too: they include Flower Power (page 111), Alphabet & Numbers (page 89), Christmas Ornaments (page 46), and the Iced gem cookies (page 122).

cutters

ducks (see page 150)
dinosaurs

recipes

1 quantity dough of your
choice makes approx.
24 little ducks and
16 dinosaurs

1 quantity Basic Royal Icing
(see page 21)

line icing

white
bright yellow

flooding icing

white

embellishments

sparkly glitter sugar
shiny colored baubles
favorite candies to make
duck jewelry

ducks

Choose your favorite colors to ice
these little rubber ducks. Decide with
your little Biscuiteers age group in mind
if you want to ice the entire body of the
duck and let it dry so they can add all
the little details, sparkles, and baubles,
or if they want to get totally involved
in the process. (See page 71 for icing
instructions.)

dinosaurs

These are really simple to ice. Using
plain white line icing, pipe on little
bones and teeth in all the right places.
Add glitter and sugars if you like, too.

Cookie Packaging

At Biscuiteers we have beautiful square-sided tins that each come with their own collection pictures on the outside. We stack the cookies on layers of crinkly cardboard, the sort you get in a box of chocolates, and sheets of beautiful colored wax paper. We secure the cookies to the card with tiny spots of line icing and then pack them snugly in layers until the tin is full. Like this they stay fresh and secure and withstand all sorts of journeys until they arrive at the door of that lucky someone who deserves a whole box of hand-iced cookies.

If you are going to send your lovingly iced cookies on a similar journey, then you need to pack yours just as carefully. Craft shops have all sorts of ideas for packaging, from handy cellophane bags to stacks of different cardboard boxes, clear plastic boxes, and tins. There are also some great opportunities to recycle packaging, too. Whatever you choose, just make sure that the cookies come in contact only with packaging that is foodsafe and clean. If you are in any doubt, wrap the cookies in cellophane or wax paper first.

If you are mailing your cookies, whatever you choose to send them in needs to be really sturdy to withstand the rigors of a postal journey. Tins and rigid boxes are perfect. Save any cookie or candy tins that you come across and look out for vintage tins in thrift shops or online. Add plenty of scrunched-up tissue paper or cellophane strands, and make sure that the cookies are protected on all sides. Or save the crinkly cardboard from boxes of chocolates, cut it to fit inside your tins, and stick the cookies to it with little spots of line icing.

If you are delivering your cookies personally, you can use more interesting packaging options. Try to think of containers that are appropriate to the design of your cookies. Pack multicolored pencil cookies into a pencil case. Pop Father's Day tool kits into a tool belt or mini toolbox. Fill a sewing basket with the Mother's Day collection. Give your teacher a pretty mug full of brightly iced paintbrushes. Using these types of container means that, after the cookies are gone, there is still a present to enjoy.

Other Ideas...

old chocolate boxes

For tiny cookies you can use empty chocolate boxes with all their packaging. Cover the outside in wrapping paper or stickers and pop a tiny cookie into each chocolate's space.

handmade envelopes

Using your cookie as a guide for size, cut out an envelope shape that will cover the cookie when all four corners are folded over. Place the cookie inside and seal the top with a sticker or tie with ribbon.

favors and little cookies

Organza or cellophane bags look lovely packed with little cookies. Place mini cookies inside and tie the top with ribbon.

cupcake cases

Stand three or four cookies in a cupcake case and tie them together with a pretty ribbon and bow.

cellophane wrapping paper

Stand the cookies carefully next to each other in a long line on a sheet of cellophane, then roll up the sides and tie up the ends with pretty ribbon or twine.

cones of paper

Make little wrapping-paper cones and either fold over the top or make a little hole and thread with ribbon. These are really lovely hanging from a Christmas or Easter tree.

cookie card

Ice your cookies in the usual way and draw around the outside of them on the front of a plain card. Draw some background details around your cookies—flowers around a butterfly, huge leaves for dinosaurs, fences and a flower bed for a new house. Then pipe a little line icing onto the card inside the outline and press the cookie down onto it to "glue" it to the paper. Allow it to dry lying down and then pop it into an envelope.

Templates

You can ice a cookie to look like pretty much any shape. If you are designing your own cookies, just remember that you can ice on much more detail than needs to be reflected in the shape of the cookie. Also bear in mind that anything too delicate will often break at some point during the baking, cooking, icing, or traveling process.

Included in this section are our favorite Biscuiteers custom cutters. To use them, simply place parchment paper over the pages and draw the outline in pencil over the shapes. If you think you will use the shape a lot, transfer the outline to thick clean cardboard (a cereal box is useful) and cut out the shape. Then use the point of a sharp knife (a scalpel available from craft shops is really good but very sharp) to cut around the template on the dough. Alternatively, place the traced outline over your dough and use the tip of a wooden skewer or toothpick in place of a pen to impress a line through the parchment onto the rolled surface. Then cut around the marks using a sharp knife as above.

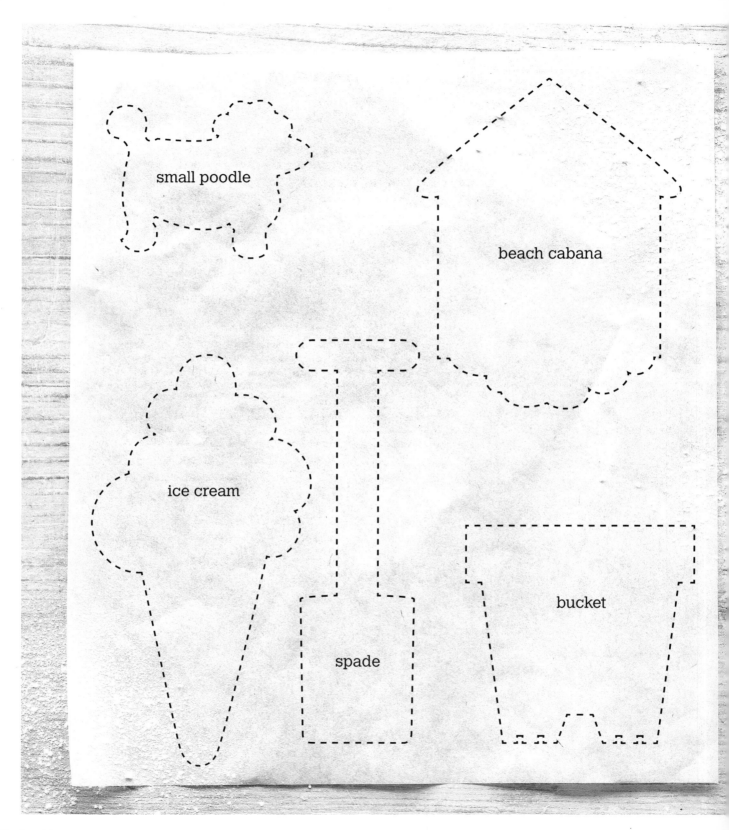

small poodle

beach cabana

ice cream

spade

bucket

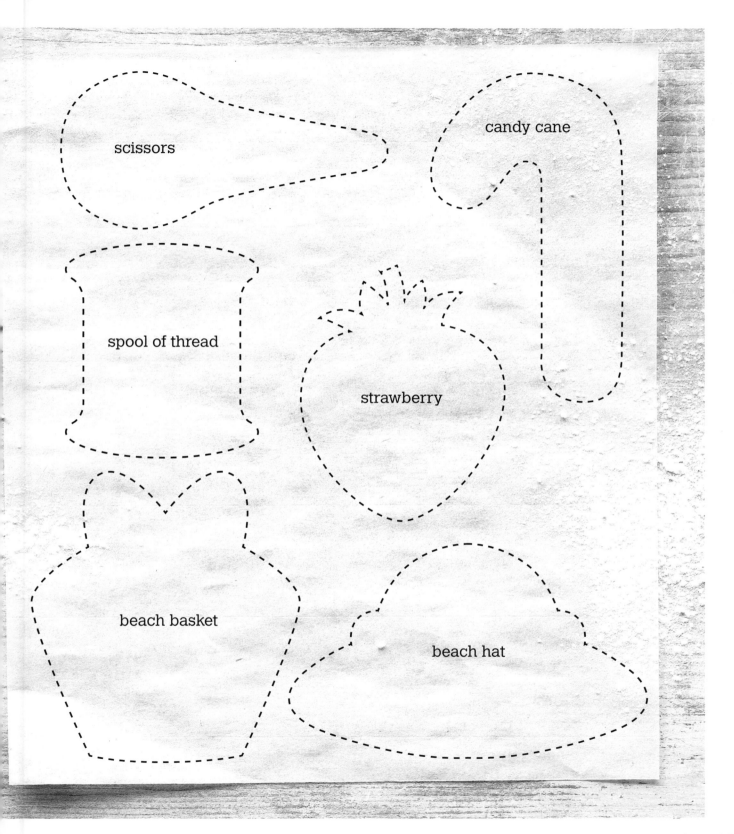

scissors

candy cane

spool of thread

strawberry

beach basket

beach hat

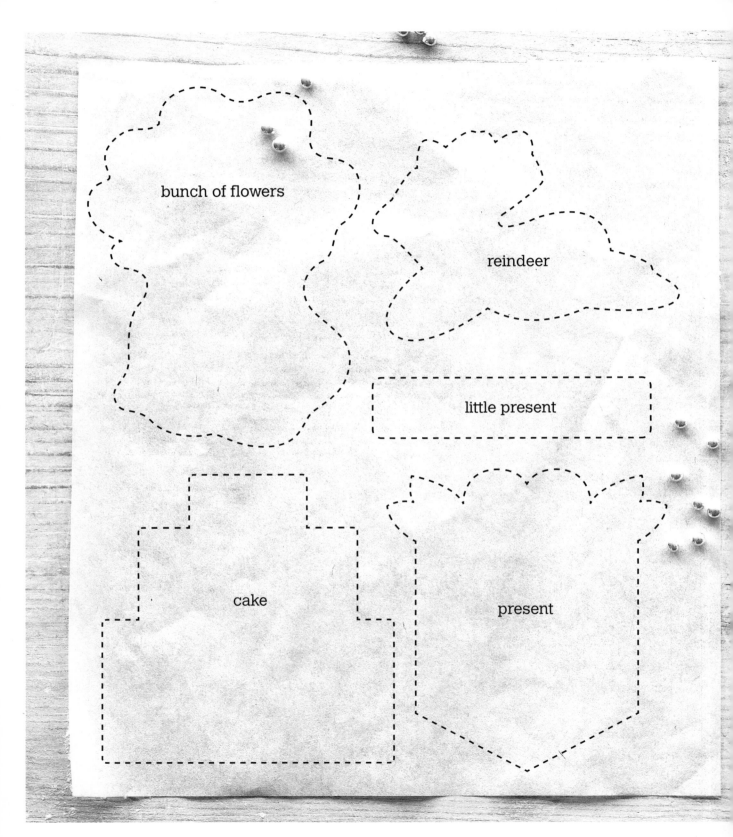

bunch of flowers

reindeer

little present

cake

present

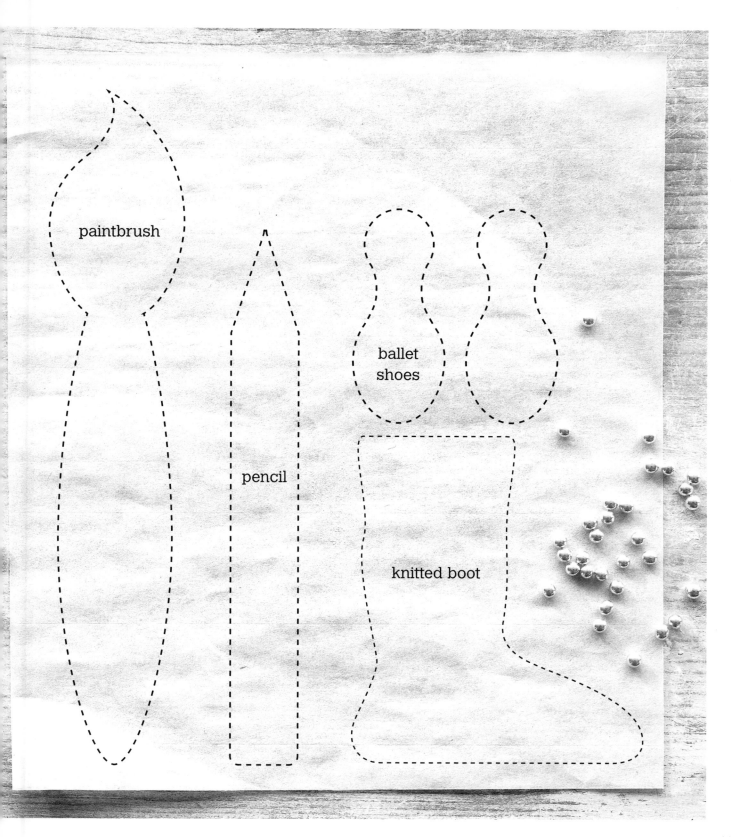

paintbrush

pencil

ballet shoes

knitted boot

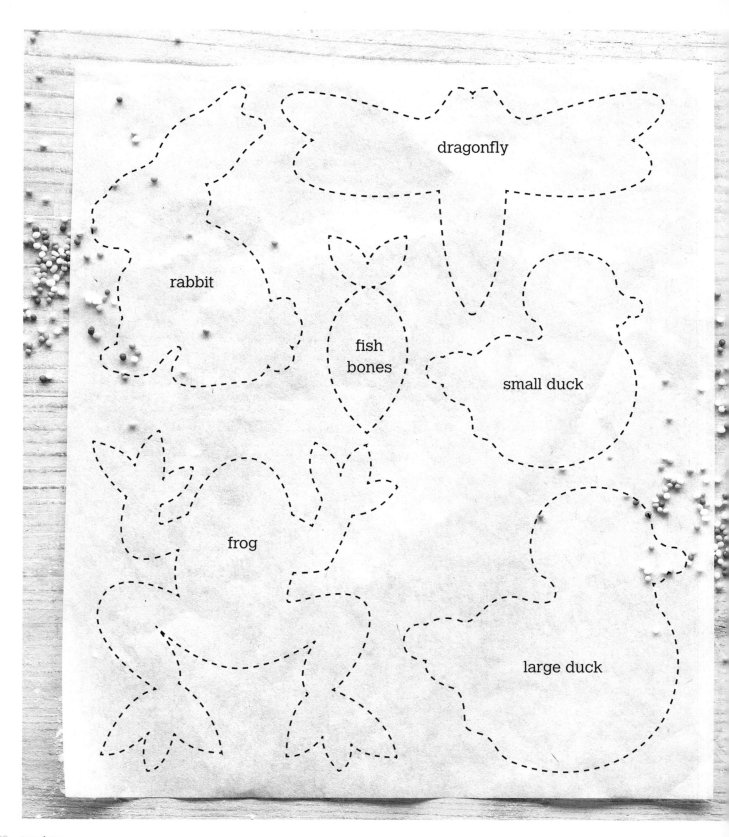

dragonfly

rabbit

fish
bones

small duck

frog

large duck

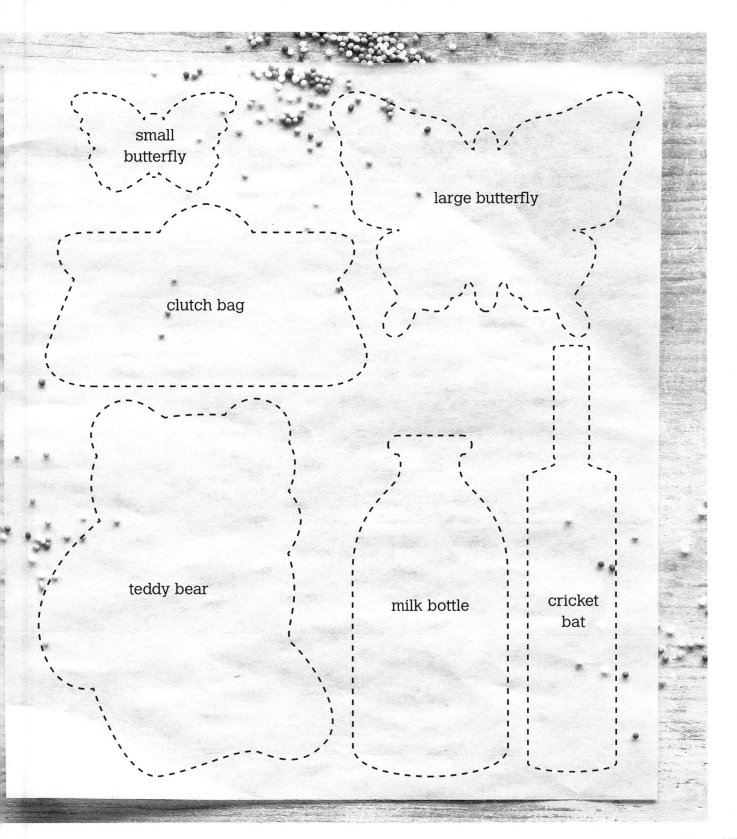

small
butterfly

large butterfly

clutch bag

teddy bear

milk bottle

cricket
bat

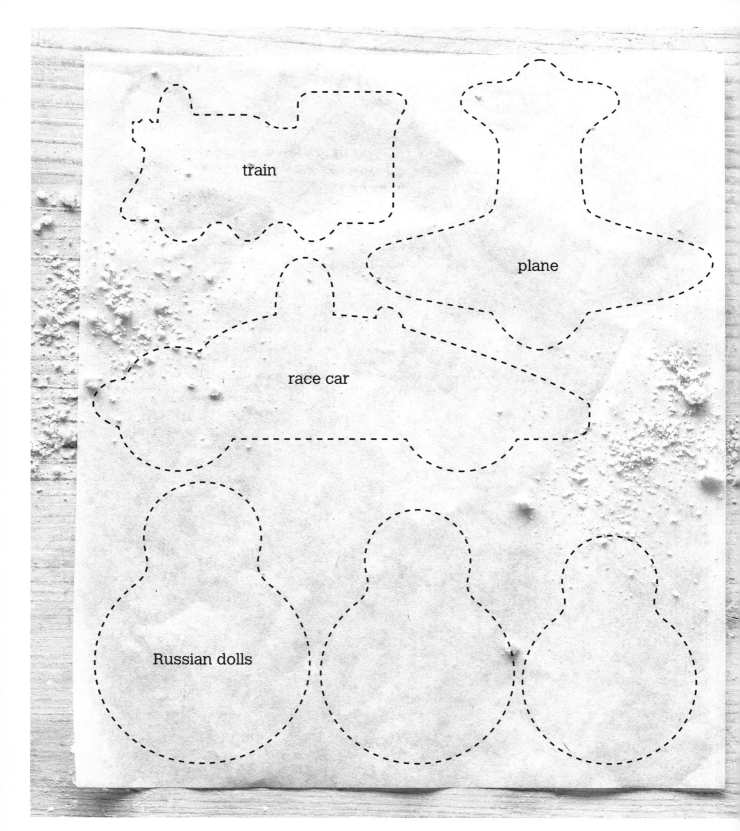

train

plane

race car

Russian dolls

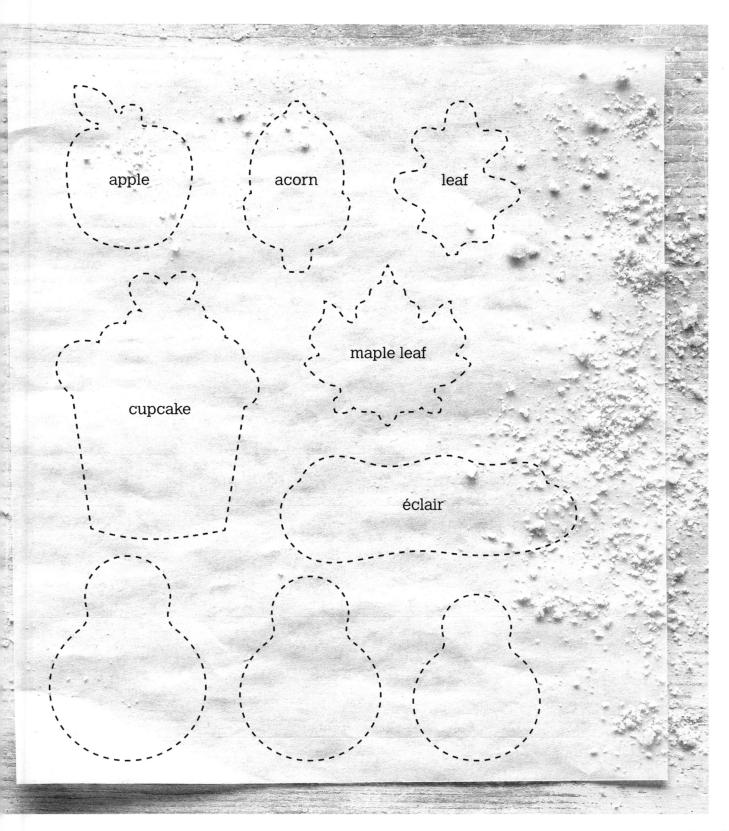

apple

acorn

leaf

cupcake

maple leaf

éclair

Equipment

- wooden spoons
- mixing bowls
- little bowls for coloring icing
- teaspoons and tablespoons
- parchment paper
- baking sheets
- cooling racks
- spatula
- offset spatula
- cutters
- sieve
- flour shaker
- rolling guides
- scales
- nozzles
- piping bags: disposable, paper, or fabric
- squeezy bottles

Suppliers

The following shops supply cookie cutters, sprinkles, and baking equipment:

Amazon.com
www.amazon.com
An excellent source for many ingredients and decorations, including gels and all types of decorations.

The Baker's Nook
902 W. Michigan, Saline, MI 48176
(734) 429-1320
www.shopbakersnook.com
A wide range of supplies from icing ingredients and decorations to cookie gift boxes.

ChefShop.com
PO Box 3488, Seattle, WA 98114
(800) 596-0885
chefshop.com
This store sells high-quality ingredients in convenient large quantities.

Country Kitchen Sweet Art
4621 Speedway Drive, Fort Wayne, IN 46825
(800) 497-3927
www.countrykitchensa.com
Edible decorations, cutters, gels, and more.

Millcreek Country Store:
Newmanstown, PA 17073
(610) 589-9492
www.millcreekcountrystore.com
All kinds of edible garnishes, such as sprinkles, nonpareils, dragées, and colored sugars.

Sugarcraft
3665 Dixie Highway, Hamilton, OH 45015
www.sugarcraft.com
Just about everything you need for making cookies, including a great selection of cutters.

Wilton Industries
2240 West 75th Street, Woodridge, IL 60517
(800) 794-5866
www.wilton.com
One-stop shopping for sugar decorations, gels, and more.

Biscuiteers Stockists:

UK
Harrods
Selfridges—London, Birmingham, Manchester
Liberty
Fortnum and Mason
Harvey Nichols
Fenwicks Newcastle

FRANCE
Colette
Le Grande Épicerie
Galeries Lafayettes

GREECE
Amadeus

DUBAI
Candylicious

Index